MONSTERS
& MYSTERIOUS
PLACES

MONSTERS
&MYSTERIOUS
PLACES

Abbeydale Press

This paperback edition published in 2008

© 1993 Bookmart Limited

ISBN: 978-1-86147-257-1

1 3 5 7 9 10 8 6 4 2

Published by Abbeydale Press
An imprint of Bookmart Limited
Registered Number 2372865
Trading as Bookmart Limited
Blaby Road, Wigston
Leicestershire, LE18 4SE

Originally incorporated in *The Encyclopedia of the
Unexplained* and *Mysteries of the Mind* published by
Bookmart Limited.

Production by Omnipress Ltd, Eastbourne

Printed in Great Britian

CONTENTS

What Lurks in the Lake?   6

Not Quite Human   26

Monsters from the Deep   44

Pagan Places, Pagan Powers   60

Celestial Signs in Sacred Places   78

The Mystic Landscape   94

A Map for the Mind   112

How Long Have They Been Here?   128

Messengers from Outer Space   148

Encounters With the Unknown   166

UFOs: The Physical Evidence   182

WHAT LURKS IN THE LAKE?

For over 1000 years there have been authenticated sightings of a monstrous creature living in one of the Earth's deepest lakes. Now scientists have finally begun to take the stories seriously, and are using state-of-the-art technology to get to the bottom of the icy black waters of Loch Ness and the secrets they hide ...

There can hardly be a person in the civilized world who has not heard of Loch Ness in Scotland and its famous monster. Possibly rather less commonly known is the fact that Nessie is but one of an army of such unexplained lake monsters. There are about 250 lakes, world-wide, which reputedly harbour creatures that, according to conventional science, should not be there – or anywhere – at all.

The first intimation that something strange might be living in Loch Ness came in St Adamnan's 7th-century biography of St Columba. In about AD 565 the latter apparently confronted a water monster living in the River Ness with the sign of the cross and so, according to Adamnan, caused it to depart the neighbourhood at speed. Over the centuries other sightings were made, although some have the curious feature that the creature was seen on land, not swimming in the Loch itself.

In 1771, for instance, one Patrick Rose saw what he described as a cross between a horse and a camel in the Looh. In 1907 (or 1919, according to some accounts) a group of local children at Invermoriston, which is about five miles from the southern end of the Loch on its western side, saw a 'light brown, camel-like quadruped' slip into the murky depths of this strange stretch of water.

A GAPING RED MOUTH

A curious event occurred in 1857 at Loch Arkaig, which is some 20 miles south-west of Loch Ness but linked to it by the same river system, so there may well be a connection of another kind with the creature reportedly living in Loch Ness.

Lord Malmesbury, a solid, bewhiskered gentleman rolled from the stoutest Victorian makings, went shooting deer near Loch Arkaig that autumn. His memoir of 3 October 1857 reads:

'This morning my stalker and his boy gave me an account of

a mysterious creature, which they say exists in Loch Arkaig, and which they call the Lake Horse. It is the same animal of which one has occasionally read accounts in newspapers as having been seen in the Highland lochs, and on the existence of which the late Lord Ellesmere wrote an interesting article…

'My stalker, John Stewart, at Achnacarry, has seen it twice, and both times at sunrise in summer on a bright sunny day, when there was not a ripple on the water. The creature was basking on the surface; he only saw the head and the hindquarters, proving that its back was hollow, which is not the shape of any fish or of a seal. Its head resembled that of a horse.'

While St Columba was in the Highlands, preaching to the Picts in the late 6th century, he chanced on a monster in the River Ness.

Local folk, then, were not unfamiliar with the presence of odd animals in the inland waters of the Highlands. Most witnesses described something with two humps, a tail, and a snake-like head. They often noted a V-shaped wash behind the creature, and commonly reported such details as a gaping red mouth and horns or antennae on the top of its head.

Children of the villages around Loch Ness were told not to go swimming in its waters lest the creatures that lived there attack them, but word of what might be in Loch Ness did not travel far. The bombshell, as far as the world outside was concerned, came in 1933. Up to a point, this has a simple, material explanation. In that year a road was dynamited into existence along the Loch's north shore, and the view across the water 'improved' by sawing away the vegetation. Tourism into the area immediately increased. So did sightings of the thing in the lake, but now they were not being made simply by local people.

'PREHISTORIC ANIMAL'

On 14 April 1933, a Mr and Mrs Mackay catapulted the Loch Ness monster into the headlines. The *Inverness Courier* reported their account of seeing an unknown creature in the Loch that 'disported itself for fully a minute, its body resembling that of a whale'. More sightings, and photographs to prove them, followed rapidly.

At 4 p.m. on 22 July 1933, Londoners Mr and Mrs George Spicer were driving along beside Loch Ness on the new road, on their way back from a holiday in northern Scotland, when their car nearly struck a huge, black creature with a long neck. The 'prehistoric animal', as Mr Spicer described it, shambled across the road, slithered through the undergrowth, and splashed into the Loch.

On 12 November 1933, an employee of the British

Aluminium Company, Hugh Gray, watched an unusually large 'object' rise out of the Loch. When it had raised itself two or three feet out of the water, Gray photographed it. He estimated the length of the thing to be about 40 ft, and described it as having greyish-coloured, smooth and shiny skin.

His photograph is, to say the least, ambiguous: it's not difficult to see in it the image of a labrador-like dog with a largish piece of wood in its mouth. But in late 1933, a little frivolity from the Highlands was good news to a world wearied by the Depression and worried by Hitler's recent rise to power. The picture was published in papers all over the globe, and the Loch Ness monster became a permanent fixture in the popular imagination. In the year after the release of the Gray photograph, there were over 50 reported sightings of 'Nessie'.

In 1934 two more photographs were taken of the creature. One was by Colonel Robert Wilson, a London doctor. Labelled the 'surgeon's picture' by the British press, Wilson's photo was clear and distinct in comparison with Gray's. It seemed to show the head and neck of a plesiosaur-like creature rising out of the water. In the summer of that year, Sir Edward Mountain organized an expedition to the Loch to investigate the stories and the sightings. A member of the group snapped a picture of something strange breaking the surface of the Loch on 13 July, but hardly any details are visible.

POMPOUS JOKE?

Since then, there have been many pictures taken of things that may or may not be mysterious animals in Loch Ness. Several have been definite hoaxes. One – taken by a notorious self-publicizing 'investigator' – was nothing more than a part-submerged fence post with a sock, or possibly a collapsed Wellington boot, stuck on top to look like the head of a monster.

The 'surgeon's picture' of Nessie, taken on 19 April 1934 by London doctor Colonel Robert Wilson, showing the classic plesiosaur-like profile of the mystery animal.

This kind of joke hardly forwards the cause of disinterested research.

Others, even some of those taken by reputable and impartial scientists, have been ambiguous at best, although not necessarily because of what they seem to show. The classic examples are the underwater pictures taken by Dr Robert H. Rines of the Academy of Applied Sciences at the renowned Massachusetts Institute of Technology during thorough surveys of the Loch in 1972 and 1975. One of the computer-enhanced photographs, taken in 1975, seems to show an animal that fits the standard description of Nessie – something rather like an aquatic dinosaur. The other, taken in 1972, apparently shows the creature's flipper.

The doubt arises not just because there is, inevitably, no background or other detail by which to judge the size of the image – Loch Ness's waters are extremely murky thanks to the amount of peat suspended in them – but because of the pompous scientific name dreamed up for the purported animal by the naturalist Sir Peter Scott. Impressed by the rhomboid shape of the flipper, Scott coined the Latin name Nessiteras rhombopteryx for the animal, a 'christening' that was taken at the time to be a sign that Nessie had been accepted into the hallowed groves of establishment science.

Then someone – who must have been either a genius with dyslexia or a fanatical crossword buff – realized that the letters of the Latin name could swiftly be rearranged to read 'Monster hoax by Sir Peter S'. Was it a joke? A revelation? A bizarre coincidence? Scott never said, while sceptics have pointed out that the image in the Rines photographs could have been of nothing more mysterious than a lump of wood.

STRIKING CONSISTENCY

If the photographic evidence is largely dubious, the circumstantial evidence that some very odd animal is alive and well and living in Loch Ness is very good. Since 1933, there have been more than 3,000 sightings of the creature. There is, to begin with, a striking consistency in reports of what people see. Most describe a long-necked, humpbacked animal that can move very fast when it wants to, whether its head is up or down, and that, at other times, will simply rise quietly to the surface for a few minutes and then sink silently below.

It is also a curious fact that apart from Loch Ness itself the worldwide sightings of lake monsters that resemble Nessie (which no living animal known to science does) have all occurred around the isothermic line of 50°F in both northern and southern hemispheres. The animal, or animals, whatever they are, thus conform to a rule of zoology in having a distinct distribution within a specific environmental pattern. They don't pop up just anywhere, and if they did there would be grounds for suspecting that they were more a figment of the imagination (or folklore) than an elusive fact of nature.

Veteran cryptozoologist Bernard Heuvelmans commented crisply: 'One could hardly wish for better circumstantial evidence for their existence.' The unanswered question remains: what might these animals actually be?

INEXHAUSTIBLE APPETITE

There are numerous theories as to the animal's identity. Candidates have included the zeuglodon, a prehistoric, snake-like primitive whale, an unknown type of long-necked seal, giant eels, and more prosaically walruses, floating mats of otters, diving birds and even – someone had to say it – mirages. A favourite contender has always been the plesiosaur, a marine reptile that has officially been extinct for the last 70 million years. The 'extinct' label affixed by science is not necessarlly proof that a species has in fact died out, however; it simply represents the current state of accepted knowledge. Until 1938 the coelacanth, a singularly ugly but otherwise inoffensive prehistoric fish, was reckoned extinct because there were no fossils of it less than 70 million years old and no living specimens had been seen; but then coelacanths were found thriving, and no doubt thoroughly indifferent to the opinions of scientists, in the Indian Ocean. So it is possible that a community of plesiosaurs has survived in the same way.

They would have had to survive in the sea for the major part of that time, but they could have found their way into Loch Ness with little or no difficulty in the last 10,000 years. Then, after the last great Ice Age ended, the glaciers retreated, and the Great Glen fault – which divides the Scottish Highlands, and of which Loch Ness is a part – opened up to the sea. On the other hand, they would have had to have adapted from being geared to a saline marine environment to survival in the fresh water of the Loch in a very short time (in evolutionary terms). But that again is not impossible.

Loch Ness is a fairly sterile place, partly because of its depth (up to an estimated 1,000 ft), its darkness, and the lack of nutrients flowing into it. But a plesiosaur could survive there on a healthy diet of fish without disturbing the Loch's basic ecosystem. At least, it could as long as it had an inexhaustible appetite for fresh salmon. This is because the mature salmon that enter the Loch from the sea, by way of the River Ness, simply don't eat, and so don't affect the rest of the food chain in the Loch. Still more convenient, salmon come into the Loch all year round, so there is a reasonably consistent and plentiful supply of food for any predator that might depend on them for survival.

THE LAST DINOSAUR?

What militates against Nessie being a leftover plesiosaur is the rarity with which it seems to appear on the surface, for the creature would have to live in the top 125 ft or so of the Loch's waters, not only because that is where the food (of any kind) is, but also because below that level the temperature drops dramatically – too low for a cold-blooded reptile (even of the 'monster's' reported size) to survive. Even the warmer level of the Loch is at the extreme end of such an animal's range. On top of that, reptiles have lungs, not gills: they need to breathe fresh air. So why aren't the 'reptiles' of Loch Ness seen on the surface more often?

The plesiosaur, which of all known animals most resembles 'typical' lake monsters, as seen in Europe and North America.

Most reptiles, too, would have to come – and stay – ashore for a brief period at least once every year to lay their eggs. No one has seen that happen yet at Loch Ness. It is, of course, again possible that the creatures move from the Loch out to the ocean for some of the year, perhaps especially in the breeding season. Nevertheless, it's surprising that this hasn't been seen happening on some rocky Scottish shore by someone at some time.

Even the possibility that the creature's elusiveness – not to say virtual invisibility – is the result of there being only a very small family of monsters in the Loch, is hardly a conclusive argument. To be viable, there would need to be a community of an average of at least three monsters alive at any one time. The

Loch's surface area is no more than 45 square miles, that is 15 square miles of surface water for every monster. The surface area of the Mediterranean is some 900,000 square miles, or 20,000 times bigger. The estimated population of the rare and endangered monk seal in the Mediterranean is between 300 and 600 or, at best, one every 1,500 square miles – 100 times the area for each Loch Ness monster. Seals are mammals and have to breathe air; they surface to do so. And they are seen every year, at all seasons, and recognized with delight for what they are, by all kinds of people all over that huge inland sea. There is no mystery about the monk seal, although they are far more sparsely distributed over a much vaster area than the extremely mysterious Loch Ness monster would seem to be.

A SWIMMING ELEPHANT?

None of that, however, is a conclusive argument against there being something – or some things – living in the Loch. It may not be a reptile at all. It may be a fish of a rather unusual variety. It may be something utterly unexpected. In August (not April!) 1979, two highly qualified academics, Dr Dennis Power and Dr Donald Johnson, suggested in the columns of the august journal *New Scientist* that the creature of Loch Ness might be a swimming elephant. While this may have started as a lighthearted article, a correspondent to *Fortean Times* gleefully pointed out a fine, ironic coincidence with this proposal. Ancient Pictish rock carvings showed (among many recognizable creatures) an animal that scholars had been unable to identify and had called either just 'the Pictish beast' or – here it comes – 'the swimming elephant'.

Certainly one of the odder aspects of the Loch Ness monster is its apparent ability to travel over land. In June 1990, retired Colonel L. McP. Fordyce published an account in *Scots*

Magazine of his experience in April 1932 – some 12 months before the event usually credited as the first 'modern' sighting of the denizen of the Loch. He too mentioned the resemblance to an elephant.

Colonel Fordyce and his wife were driving south in their six-cylinder Morris Isis, along the minor road on the south side of the Loch from Foyers to Fort Augustus. At one point the road leaves the shoreline and winds through woodland. Colonel Fordyce wrote:

'Travelling at about 25 mph in this wooded section, we were startled to see an enormous animal coming out of the woods on our left and making its way over the road about 150 yards ahead of us, towards the loch.

'It had the gait of an elephant, but looked like a cross between a very large horse and a camel, with a hump on its back and a small head on a long neck.'

Colonel Fordyce was not a soldier for nothing. He got out of his car and followed the animal on foot 'for a short distance. From the rear it looked grey and shaggy. Its long, thin neck gave it the appearance of an elephant with its trunk raised.'

THE MONSTER BITES BACK

So, the mystery deepens and, in its way, becomes almost as murky as the peat-ridden waters of the Loch itself. But one of the most persuasive arguments that a large, strange animal of some kind is living in (or near) Loch Ness is the variety of different traditions and sightings from other, similar lakes around the world that share certain geographic and topographical features with Loch Ness. For the mystery animals are all reported from lake and river systems that either are connected to the sea or have been in the past, and they all either harbour or once harboured migratory fish. Many of the lakes that fit this pattern are also deep and cold.

One such is Lake Storsjön in central Sweden, which is connected by river systems to the Gulf of Bothnia, a spur of the Baltic Sea. For 350 years or more there have been reports of a monster in the lake, and since 1987 alone the local Society for Investigating the Chat Lake has collected over 400 reports of sightings. Few, unfortunately, are consistent, so there is no clear idea of what the creature might really look like. Some witnesses have seen an animal with a large neck that undulates back and forth and looks like a horse's mane. Others described a large worm-like creature with distinct 'ears' on its head. According to reports, the beast's size may vary from 10 to 42 ft in length.

By a brilliant irony, one famous sighting was made by a local fisheries conversation officer, Ragnar Bjorks. The 73-year-old official was out checking fishing permits among anglers on the lake in the 1970s when he had the fright of his life. A huge tail suddenly broke the calm surface near Bjorks's 12 ft rowing boat. The creature that owned the tail seemed to be 18 ft long, and was grey-brown on top with a yellow underbelly. Bjorks struck at it with his oar and hit it on the back. The creature reacted by slapping the water mightily with its tail: Bjorks and his boat were ignominiously hurled about 10 ft in the air. During his brief flight Bjorks became a convinced believer in lake monsters.

WAKING VENGEANCE

Inconsistent reports also come from Ireland, where in Connemara a wilderness of rocks and peatbog is broken up by a patchwork of loughs of all sizes. Here, as in the Highlands of Scotland, it's possible that the unidentified denizens of the loughs move from one to another. Such migration would help explain why so many very small stretches of water in Connemara seem to house so many animals and such large ones to boot. But there seem to be several kinds of the creatures, if the witnesses' reports are accurate.

In the evening of 22 February 1968 farmer Stephen Coyne and his son were gathering peat beside Lough Nahooin, a tiny peat tarn, only some 100 by 80 yds in extent, near Gladdaghduff. Alerted to something weird in the water by the behaviour of their dog, Coyne sent the boy to fetch the rest of his family to watch it. The seven-strong family were joined by four other local children.

They agreed that the creature was probably about 12 ft long, hairless, with 'eel-like' black skin. It had a 'pole-like' neck, in diameter about 12 in, and apparently horns on its head that may have been protuberances housing its eyes, and a pale mouth. When it put its head underwater two humps showed above the surface. The group caught only glimpses of a tail.

This is entirely different from the animal spotted in Lough Dubh, another small lake in County Galway, near Glinsk. Three men saw a monster there in 1956, and in 1960 three of them were seen in the lough. One day in March 1962, schoolteacher Alphonsus Mullaney and his son Alphonsus Jr went fishing there for pike, and took rod and line stout enough to handle these hefty fish. Mullaney caught more than a fish:

'Suddenly there was a tugging on the line. I thought it might be on a root, so I took it gently. It did not give. I hauled it slowly ashore, and the line snapped. I was examining the line when the lad screamed.

'Then I saw the animal. It was not a seal or anything I had ever seen. It had for instance short thick legs, and a hippo face. It was as big as a cow or an ass, square faced? with small ears and a white pointed horn on its snout. It was dark grey in colour, and covered with bristles or short hair, like a pig.'

19

The thing, hurt and furious, was trying to get out of the water and wreak vengeance on its hapless fishers. Mullaney and his son fled. A posse of local men later returned with guns to search for the creature, but they found nothing. Nothing like it has been reported since from Lough Dubh.

Different again was the monster seen in Lough Auna, three miles or so north-east of Clifden, the 'capital' of Connemara. Air Commodore Kort, who had moved to Ireland after retiring from the Royal Netherlands Air Force, was about to go indoors at the end of a barbecue party in the summer of 1980 when he and one of his guests saw what seemed to be the sawtooth, reptilian dorsal fin of an animal moving slowly across the lough. The fin was about 5 ft long and stood 12 in out of the water. 'The uncanny thing about it,' said Kort, 'was the gliding movement without any disturbance of the water on the surface.'

WATER SERPENT

In North America, monsters such as the frequently seen but so far unidentified inhabitant of New Brunswick's Lake Utopia and 'Manipogo' of Lake Manitoba in Canada, and those of Lake Erie (where there were many sightings in 1991) and Hathead Lake in Montana, were all locally renowned long before 'Nessie' grabbed the world's headlines.

One such lives in the 109-mile long Lake Champlain, which adjoins New York State, Vermont and Quebec. Lake Champlain's monster, nicknamed 'Champ', has been sighted over 240 times, nearly half of them since 1982. The first really detailed report came in July 1883. The Sheriff of Clinton County, New York, Captain Nathan H. Mooney, was on the north-west arm of the lakeshore when he saw a huge water serpent about 50 yds from him. The creature rose about 5 ft out of the water, which was rough. He reckoned the animal was 25 or 30 ft long.

Its neck was about 7 in in diameter, with visibly contracting muscles, and was curved like that 'of a goose when about to take flight'. Mooney noted that there were round white spots inside the creature's mouth.

Candidates for the identity of 'Champ' are identical to those offered for the Loch Ness monster, with the plesiosaur leading.

There are a number of photographs of the creature. Perhaps the most significant was taken on 5 July 1977 by Sandra Mansi of Connecticut, who described the thing as a 'dinosaur' with its neck and head some 6 ft out of the water. The Mansi photograph has been examined by scientists and declared to be a genuine original of something in the water. But what?

An early effort to trap the creature of Loch Ness – a huge steel cage, built in 1933.

THE 'REMORSEFUL ONE'

The best-known Canadian lake monster, 'Ogopogo' of British Columbia's Lake Okanagan, also made its debut long before Nessie. Reports go back to 1850, although the local Indians were familiar with the beast long before that, and indeed named it the 'remorseful one'. Indian legend says the creature was once human – a murderer turned into a serpent as punishment for his crimes. In 1926, the editor of the *Vancouver Sun* wrote of the creature: 'Too many reputable people have seen it to ignore the seriousness of actual facts.'

A recent sighting shows how witnesses are convinced that there is indeed something odd in Lake Okanagan. In the summer of 1989, hunting guide Ernie Giroux and his wife were standing on the banks of the lake when an animal about 15 ft long surfaced from the calm waters and swam 'real gracefully and fast', as Giroux later told reporters. The creature had a round head 'like a football'. Several feet of the creature's neck and body came up out of the water. The Girouxs saw the monster at the same spot where, a few weeks before, British Columbian car salesman Ken Chaplin had taken a video of what he described as a dark green, snake-like creature about 15 ft long.

Wildlife experts who saw the video said the animal was more likely a beaver or a large river otter than a 'monster'. Ernie Giroux was unimpressed.

'I've seen a lot of animals swimming in the wild and what we saw that night was definitely not a beaver,' he said bluntly.

At the other end of the Americas is 'Nahuelito', the denizen of Nahuel Huapi Lake at the foot of the Patagonian mountains in southern Argentina. The lake, which covers 318 square miles, is in a popular resort area. Dozens of tourists and local people have seen the creature.

Accounts of the animal vary. Some describe a giant water snake with humps and fish-like fins; others speak of a swan with a snake's head, while yet others liken it to the overturned hull of a boat or a tree stump. Estimates of the creature's length range from 15 to 150 ft. 'Nahuelito' seems to surface only in the summer, when the wind is still. A sudden swell of water and a shooting spray usually precede a sighting.

Patagonia, mountainous and desolate at best, has long been the source of tales of monstrous animals, and even human giants. Patagonian Indians told the first colonists of a huge lake-dwelling creature without head, legs or tail. The rumoured existence of a Patagonian plesiosaur was given additional fuel in the early 1920s, when a gold prospector named Sheffield followed an unusual spoor and found a bizarre water beast at the end of the trail:

'I saw in the middle of the lake,' he reported, 'an animal with a huge neck like that of a swan, and the movement in the water made me suppose the beast to have a body like that of a crocodile.' An expedition, led by Dr C. Onelli, Director of the Buenos Aires Zoo, set out to catch or photograph the animal, but sadly failed.

THE LATEST TECHNOLOGIES

What would solve the mystery of the world's lake monsters?

Naturalists are agreed that only the capture of a live specimen or the discovery of a carcass (scientists tend to disapprove of investigators 'acquiring' dead specimens by ballistic means) would admit the monsters into the charmed circle of conventional science. But hunting lake monsters is not the world's easiest task. No live monsters have been caught, yet.

No carcasses have been found either that might be anything other than recognizable animals. Dead specimens may be elusive because the typical monster haunt is a very deep lake. A dead monster would sink to the bottom, where the water pressure would slow down the rate of decomposition – leaving time for eels and other creatures to consume the remains.

Giant nets, submarines, underwater cameras, sonar, lake and loch-side crews of observers have all failed to come up with unambiguous and unimpeachable evidence that would prove to the world that there is an actual monster in any of their reputed haunts. If the animals as reported do exist, they are quite possibly frightened away by the sounds made by the very devices that are being used to track them – as well as by engine noise from the boats.

Probably the best and most famous search of all was 'Operation Deepscan' which took place in 1987. The plan was to sweep the whole length of the Loch with a sonar curtain, using the world's most sophisticated sonar equipment – the Lowrance X-16 Computer Graph Recorder. Although the main goal of the search was to gather as much data as possible about the structure and ecology of the Loch, the world was watching in the hope they would prove the existence of an age-old legend – the Loch Ness monster.

After years of careful planning, the operation was launched on a clear autumn day. Twenty-four boats, all equipped with a Lowrance X-16, positioned themselves across the one-mile (1.6-km) width of the Loch. They moved slowly across the surface of the entire 23-mile (37-km) length of the Loch which, in many places, is over 700 feet (213 meters) deep and then repeated the whole process again. During this two-day search, there were several strong sonar 'contacts', all of which appeared to be moving. However, the one that was of prime interest was one that appeared at around 606 feet (185 meters). It was estimated that the object could have been about 50 lb (22.6 kg) in weight, far less than the estimated 2,500 lb

Operation Deepscan in 1987 was a massive attempt to 'catch' Nessie. A score or so of launches equipped with sonar detectors made a sweep of the entire Loch. Such a method may, however, have succeeded only in frightening any animals below into hiding.

(1,134 kg) of Nessie. Was it Nessie the Loch Ness monster? There was little evidence to confirm it – and yet neither is there absolute and positive proof that it was not.

But until that solid evidence turns up, these strange animals will remain classic mysteries. And credible witnesses will continue to report them, take fuzzy photographs, and keep the lake monster legends alive and swimming.

NOT QUITE HUMAN

As he began his descent down the mountain through the heavy mist, the professor thought he was hearing the echo of his footsteps. Terror seized him when he realized that the footsteps belonged to something different – to something malignant…

Abominable snowmen and other horrid hairy man-beasts are strictly contained in the Himalayas, the wilderness of the USA, and the remoter parts of China. Or so you thought.

At 4,296 ft Ben MacDhui is the highest peak in Scotland's Cairngorm mountains, and the second highest in the country. Many who have scaled Ben MacDhui are convinced that a malignant entity – which locals call Am Fear Liath Mor, the Big Grey Man – lives on the mountain.

The first report from anyone outside the area that something sinister haunted Ben MacDhui came in December 1925 at the Annual General Meeting of the Cairngorm Club. Professor Norman Collie told his suitably astonished audience that in 1891 he had been climbing through heavy mist down from the summit of Ben MacDhui, when, he said, 'I began to think I heard something else than merely the noise of my own footsteps. For every few steps I took I heard a crunch, and then another crunch as if someone was walking after me but taking steps three or four times the length of my own.'

At first he thought his imagination was working overtime, but the sound persisted, although whatever was making it remained hidden in the mist. Then, as the eerie crunching continued, Collie said, 'I was seized with terror and took to my heels, staggering blindly among the boulders for four or five miles.'

Collie vowed never to return to the mountain alone, and remained convinced that there was 'something very queer about the top of Ben MacDhui'.

His chilling account was soon picked up by the newspapers, with the result that other mountaineers came forward to record that they too had had similar experiences of uncontrollable and inexplicable fear and panic while on Ben MacDhui. Some had barely managed to avoid lethal falls in their compulsion to get away as quickly as possible from the terrifying presence.

This sounds like a paranormal presence, but some

witnesses have actually seen the thing, reporting a huge, man-like figure, and many accounts mention the same heavy footsteps with the unusually long stride that Collie heard.

Plenty of explanations have been put forward for these experiences. They range from the presence of yeti-like man-beasts and optical illusions to the (inevitable) 'base for extraterrestrial aliens' and (more plausibly) hallucinations brought on by lack of oxygen. This latter most probably accounts for some of the more exotic reports of the Big Grey Man, which mention strains of ghostly music and sepulchral laughter wafting across the mountain during its appearance.

But leaving the wonkier propositions aside does not mean dumping the 'man-beast' explanation entirely. There is a long tradition that hairy man-beasts inhabited the British mainland in the past. Known as 'woodwoses', or more mundanely as 'wild men of the woods', their images can be seen carved into the decorations in many old East Anglian churches. There is not much forest on Ben MacDhui, and it is a long way from East Anglia, but the possibility that a colony of these legendary creatures has survived in Scotland remains to tantalize the imagination.

FOUL ODOURS

Although conventional zoology says that one wouldn't expect to find apes of any kind, let alone 'ape men', living in South America or Australia, any more than in the British Isles, both continents can boast plenty of eyewitnesses who would swear that the contrary is true and that the scientists are wrong.

Australia's man-beast is known as the 'yowie'. Most reports have come from New South Wales and Queensland, and the creatures have been seen by settlers since the mid-19th century at least. The Aborigines have known about them since

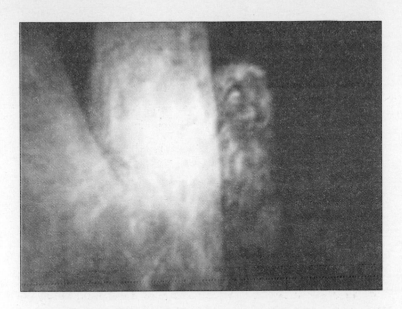

The first recorded sighting of an Australian 'yowie' by a European came in 1881, when an Australian newspaper reported that several witnesses had seen a large baboon-like animal that stood taller than a man. This image was captured on video by a man who claimed to have seen the monster.

long before then. Like North America's 'bigfoot' and 'sasquatch', the yowie can remain remarkably unperturbed when surprised. When George Summerell, who was riding a horse, came upon one bending down to drink from a creek near Bemboka, New South Wales, on 12 October 1912, it simply 'rose to its full height, of aboul 7 feet, and looked quietly at the horseman', according to an item in the *Sydney Morning Herald*. 'Then stooping down again, it finished its drink, and then, picking up a stick that lay by it, walked steadily away... and disappeared among the rocks and timber 150 yards away.'

Footprints around the shore of the creek showed that the

creature had been there at least a fortnight before, as well, and that the animal had only four toes – a feature of other man-beast prints taken around the world. But the yowie has two other features commonly reported by witnesses of the North American man-beasts: no neck, and the ability to emit revolting smells at will. In early 1978, an Australian National Parks worker was cutting timber near Springbrook in Queensland when he saw 'this big black hairy man-thing' about 12 ft away from him.

'It had huge hands,' he said, 'and... a flat, black shiny face, with two big yellow eyes and a hole for a mouth. It just stared at me and I stared back. I was so numb I couldn't even raise the axe I had in my hand. We [were] staring at each other for about 10 minutes before it suddenly gave off a foul smell that made me vomit – then it just made off sideways and disappeared.'

THE BEASTS ATTACK

The most intriguing and controversial encounter with a South American man-beast took place along the Tarra river on the Venezuela–Colombia border in 1920. A 20-strong team of geological surveyors, led by Swiss geologist Dr François de Loys, had set out in 1917 but at the end of three years had been reduced to a handful by disease, venomous animals, and the poisoned arrows of hostile Indians. One day in 1920, this ragged band saw coming through the foliage ahead of them two 5 ft tall, ape-like but tail-less creatures, walking upright on their hind legs.

When the beasts – one male and the other female – saw the geologists, they became plainly agitated, tearing angrily at the vegetation around them. They got so excited that both defecated into their hands and flung their excrement at the scientists. Then they moved forward – as if to attack, it seemed to the geologists, who responded with a hail of small-arms fire. The female died instantly. The male fled.

The geologists examined the carcass, noted its details, and photographed it. Most of the pictures were lost when the party's boat capsized later in the expedition, but one survived. On returning to Europe, De Loys showed it to the French anthropologist Professor George Montandon. He was convinced that it showed a species comparable to the Old World's apes – chimpanzees, gorillas, orang-utans and gibbons. He formally named it Ameranthropoides loysi – 'Loys's American ape'. Other scientists were less impressed.

The creature did look somewhat like an oversized and tailless spider monkey, and most zoologists maintained that it was some form of spider monkey. Some even hinted, none too subtly, at a hoax. Montandon answered all the criticisms in painstaking detail, but his critics were unmoved: as far as establishment science was concerned, De Loys's find was not an ape, and the issue was soon simply ignored.

But there is plenty of circumstantial evidence in favour of creatures like the one De Loys shot and photographed. Indian tribes in the jungles all over South America have long believed in the existence of ape-like beasts that walk upright and lack tails. And among the ruins of various South American and Mexican ancient cities are sculptures of gorilla-like creatures quite unlike any known New World primate – but they do resemble the South American ape woman shot by De Loys's party. Further, there is no ecological reason why such an ape should not be able to survive in the South American environment – but conventional science always prefers to ignore awkward little questions and hairsplitting logic like that.

OUT OF AFRICA

In contrast to the areas we've looked at so far, it would make sense if hairy man-beasts were to be found living in Africa.

Apart from its vast areas of wilderness in which such creatures could roam free, with little risk of being detected by people, the continent is now known to be the 'cradle of mankind' – the place where humans, Homo sapiens, evolved.

The oldest African fossils of hominids are the australopithecines, which first appeared over three million years ago. Some types were notably slender, others more robust – and so it is just possible that these or other ancient evolutionary forms, somewhere between apes and men, have survived out of sight in Africa to this day. And if one goes by the huge dossier of eyewitness reports, Africa is indeed home to an enormous variety of unidentified man-beasts.

Living specimens of slender australopithecine would look like several unidentified man-beasts as witnesses have described them. Among these are Zaire's 'kakundakari', the 'fating'ho' of Senegal, and Tanzania's 'agogwe'. According to witnesses, the agogwe is small, russet-furred and man-like, and sometimes mixes with other primates such as baboons. Elders of the Mandinka tribe of Senegal speak of the fating'ho as if it were just as real as any of the known animals inhabiting their lands, though it is rarely seen nowadays (perhaps simply because it has become rarer).

Other man-beasts seem to resemble the robust species of australopithecines. Among these are the 'kikomba' of Zaire, and Sudan's 'wa'ab'. These may even be surviving examples of humanity's direct evolutionary ancestor, Homo erectus.

The French anthropologist Jacqueline Roumeguere-Eberhardt has concluded that there are no less than five different species of man-beast living in Kenya. She has cautiously dubbed them 'X One' through to 'X Five'.

X One is a typical bigfoot-like being, hairy, huge, and possibly social, since it's been seen carrying buffalo meat rather than gorging it on the spot. It also defends itself with a kind of

The enigmatic female beast shot by members of a geological survey team led by François de Loys on the Venezuela-Colombia border in 1920. Controversy still rages over the true nature of the creature.

33

sardonic gentleness. A young hunter who was cornered by the beast said it simply removed his arrows from their quiver, broke them up and put them back.

X Two is a cave-dwelling creature with a hairless, beige-coloured body with curly black hair on its head. A noticeably humanoid beast, it is tall and thin, and seems to live in nuclear families.

X Three is tall, and uses tools for hunting. Males have been seen to fell buffalo 'with an uprooted tree with its roots carved into spikes'. The beast then wields 'a spear-like knife' to cut out its prey's internal organs, 'which are then eaten on the spot'.

X Four is a hairy-chested, fat-bodied pygmy-like hominoid that, witnesses say, is often to be seen carrying a digging stick which it uses to uproot tubers.

X Five is exclusively vegetarian, a man-beast that carries bows and arrows and is apparently capable of making leatherwork bags.

Despite the wealth of sightings of African man-beasts, no one has yet caught or killed one, or found a skeleton that would provide conclusive proof of their existence. But Africa has given zoologists plenty of surprises in the 20th century alone. As the saying goes, 'There is always something new out of Africa.' So, perhaps, as the English cryptozoologist Dr Karl Shuker has put it, the most secretive of continents may be saving its most sensational surprise for the future.

THE INCREDIBLE HULK?

As far as the West is concerned, the granddaddy of all hairy man-beasts is, of course, the so-called 'abominable snowman' or 'yeti' of the Himalayas. The existence of what, correctly translated, the local people call 'a man-like living thing that is not a human being' first came to the West's attention in 1921, when Lt Col C.K. Howard-Bury was surveying Mt Everest for a forthcoming attempt to reach the summit. On 22 September that year he came across huge footprints on a snowfield where, earlier, he had seen dark, man-like forms moving around. News of these two events sped round the world, and have been reinforced by sightings from virtually every mountaineering expedition into the area since.

The term 'abominable snowman' is not only a mistranslation of the Nepalese term for these creatures – it's irritatingly misleading. There seems to be nothing particularly abominable about the yeti, and they appear on the high Himalayan snowfields only when making their way from one hot and humid valley, where they seem to spend most of their time, to another. And the term also implies that there is only one of these creatures. Not only are there many individuals, if reports are to be trusted, but there are at least three different kinds of yeti.

The word yeti itself is a Sherpa term that means, roughly, 'That-thing-there'. Investigator (and oil millionaire) Tom Slick was the first to conclude, from his expeditions to the Himalayas in 1957 and 1958, that there were at least two types of creature that local people had seen.

The 'original' yeti is the *meh-teh*, a man-sized creature that sports a conical head set on a stout neck, with a jutting jaw and a wide, lipless mouth. The body is covered in thick, reddish-brown fur. Prints show short, broad feet. Meh-teh eat plants and small animals, including birds, which they hunt in the upper forests of the mountains.

There is also a pygmy man-beast of the Himalayas, *teh-lma*, which means 'man-like being'. Standing about 3–4 ft tall, these creatures live deeper in the valleys than meh-teh, surviving on a diet largely of frogs and insects. Their thick fur is dark red, with a slight mane on the back.

The third species of yeti is known in the Himalayas, but only by repute. Called *dzu-teh* – 'hulking living thingy' – these beasts are huge, far taller and bulkier than a human, with a dark shaggy coat, a flat head with beetling brows, long powerful arms and hands, and large feet that leave prints with two pads under the first toe, which points out and away from the others on the foot. They live not in the Himalayas but in eastern Tibet and northern China, on a mainly vegetarian diet.

This matter of the two pads (and other features) showing in the dzu-teh's footprint is important, and so is the animal's habitat. American cryptozoologist Loren Coleman first pointed out that both plant and animal species in the areas of China where dzu-teh (called 'yeren' in China) are consistently reported bear an uncanny resemblance – they are often related to, or the same as – those found in the Pacific Northwest of North America. And this is where bigfoot and sasquatch are most often seen. And the footprints of yeren and bigfoot are strikingly similar in the configuration of their pads, ridges and disposition of the toes.

ALMOST HUMAN

So, are bigfoot (alias sasquatch) and yeren (alias dzu-teh) related – or even separate communities of the same animal? And if so, what animal?

The favourite candidate is a species of giant ape, named Gigantopithecus, which lived in southern China until it, apparently, became extinct 500,000 years ago. Its anatomy is somewhere between ape and human. Gigantopithecus, as its name implies, was huge. Males probably weighed around 806 lb and females around 500 lb. This is easily the largest primate that ever lived. Gigantopithecus also, almost certainly, stood and walked in a human manner.

Humans and all apes share a unique set of anatomical

traits in the arms, shoulders, and thorax, since all evolved to swing through trees. Humans gave up this form of personal transport long ago, preferring walking horse-riding and eventually the Ford Model T. As a result they lost their tails. Gigantopithecus also belonged to this group of higher primates, but it was too large to swing through trees, and probably, therefore, also lost its tail. Its wide chest, broad shoulders, and lack of tail would make it conspicuous among apes – and remarkably like a human in appearance.

Gigantopitheces had an ape-like face and was covered with

A frame from the famous movie of a bigfoot filmed by Roger Patterson on 20 October 1967 at Bluff Creek in northern California. Expert opinion says the film was not faked.

body hair. Their faces would have had the ape's retreating forehead and blunt nose, but with a more human set to the mouth and jaw. They did not make tools and had less-than-human intelligence. They probably did not live in close social groups. All these features are remarkably consistent with the reported appearance and behaviour of bigfoot/sasquatch.

Most authorities presume that Gigantopithecus is extinct because the most recent fossil teeth (from northern Vietnam) are 300,000 years old. Other finds date back a million years. But one early Gigantopithecus jaw from India is at least five million years old. Thus, the animals survived for four million years although we have no direct physical evidence that they did. So they could have survived during the 300,000 years since the owner of the most recent fossil remains died off and still leave no sign of being here.

'I RAN OUT OF FILM'

Although many American Indian tribes of the Pacific Northwest tell tales of bigfoot, and in them treat the creature just as they do less elusive animals, it was not until 1958 that the American public at large became aware of the bigfoot phenomenon. In the summer of 1958 strange, giant footprints cropped up around some road-making equipment at Bluff Creek in northern California. The tracks appeared several nights in a row, alarming the workers who found them. Once the major San Francisco papers picked up the story, it soon got national attention. Bigfoot had become the ultimate reclusive media star.

The next major sighting, which also netted a major piece of evidence, came in 1967. On 20 October that year Roger Patterson and Bob Gimlin of Yakima, Washington, went to Bluff Creek in the hope of catching sight of a bigfoot after hearing that tracks had been seen again in the area. They went on horseback, and were

40 or 50 miles from the nearest road when they rounded a bend on the trail and came to a creek. In Gimlin's words: 'Here this thing stood by the creek, just stood. We were on one side of the creek, the creature on the other and our horses went crazy. Roger's little horse just went bananas.'

Patterson managed to haul out the 16-mm movie camera, loaded with colour film, that he was carrying in his saddlebag.

'This creature turned,' said Gimlin, 'and started to walk away from us, just slow like a man would if he were just walking down the street, but as it did this, Roger ran across the creek behind it, but then he stumbled on a sandbar... He was shooting the camera while he was running. He hollered back for me when he stumbled and fell. He said, "Cover me!" and, naturally, I knew what he meant.

'So I rode across the creek on my horse and took my .30-06 rifle out of the saddle scabbard and just stood there (pointing but not aiming the rifle at the beast). When I did this, this creature was... about 90 feet [away] – and it turned and looked at me; just turned as it was walking away. It never stopped walking. And then... I heard Roger say, "Oh my God, I ran out of film."'

Gimlin remains adamant that he and Patterson saw a genuine bigfoot that day. Two things support his contention. First, Patterson is now dead, and Gimlin has more to gain financially from a confession to a hoax than stoutly maintaining the opposite – after all, he owns no rights in the film.

Second, the oft-mentioned possibility that a third party hoaxed the two bigfoot-hunters seems highly unlikely. To begin with, such a prankster would have had to have anticipated the pair's moves over many miles of rough country, seeing them but not being seen. Even if the hypothetical hoaxer had managed that feat of fieldcraft, only an idiot would risk getting in the way of a shot from Gimlin's powerful hunting rifle; the .30-06 round will bring down a bear.

And some expert scientific opinion backs the men's claim. One expert who studied the film, Dmitri Donskoy, Professor of Biomechanics at the Soviet Central Institute of Physical Culture in Moscow, noted that the creature's gait was that of an animal with enormous weight and strength, and that the movement of the whole body was fluid and confident. 'These factors... allow us to evaluate the gait of the creature as a natural movement without any sign of the artfulness that one would see in an imitation,' he concluded. 'At the same time, with all the diversity of locomotion illustrated by the creature of the footage, its gait as seen is absolutely non-typical of man.'

Another expert, Donald Grieve, Reader in Biomechanics at the Royal Free Hospital in London, was similarly impressed, but had a reservation. He felt that if the camera speed – which Patterson did not know for sure – had been set at 24 frames per second, the film could be showing a large, walking man. But if the film had been shot at 18 frames per second, no human being would be able to match the movements shown. He concluded with rare honesty: 'My subjective impressions have oscillated between total acceptance of the Bigfoot on the grounds that the film would be difficult to fake, to one of irrational rejection based on an emotional response to the possibility that the Bigfoot actually exists.'

The leading US authority on bigfoot, Professor Grover Krantz of Washington State University, made a detailed analysis of the movie in 1991, and concluded that it was indeed shot at 18 frames per second. The animal's movements, he believes, were impossible for a human to imitate, and convincingly show the creature's massiveness and strength. And he noted that its huge size, and muscles to match, were well outside the normal range of human variation. In other words, if Patterson's bigfoot had been a man in a fur suit, he would have been a giant who had pumped an awful lot of iron.

DEAD OR ALIVE

More impressive evidence for the reality of bigfoot comes from a set of footprints that were discovered and cast by US Forest Service workers in 1982, in the Blue Mountains along the Washington–Oregon border. The prints were made in very fine soil that was slightly damp. All the casts show ridges on the skin under the toes and on the soles. These are just like fingerprints, and only the palms and soles of higher primates have them. Forty police fingerprinters have studied these casts over the years, and have all concluded that the footprints must have been made by one or more genuine bigfeet.

As shown by this artist's impression, bigfoot towers over an average-sized man.

Opinion among anthropologists and primatologists who have seen the casts is mixed. Many suggested that the casts had been made from human footprints that had somehow been enlarged – a latex mould of a footprint will expand by 50 per cent when soaked in kerosene. This trick also expands the spacing between the ridges by 50 per cent. All the fingerprint experts noted that the ridges on these footprints were spaced just like those on the skin of other primates.

Despite all this circumstantial evidence, the only thing that will convince mainstream science of the reality of bigfoot will be part or all of a specimen itself, dead or alive. Professor Krantz remarks that 'a single lower jaw would be enough to establish not only its existence, but whether Gigantopithecus is still with us'.

INFESTED WATERS

Bigfoot is by no means the only mystery man-beast in North America, nor the strangest. The prize for the most bizarre has to go to a nightmarish creature nicknamed Lizard Man.

Witnesses describe it as 7 ft tall, walking upright like a man – but with green scaly skin, glowing red eyes, three toes on each foot and three fingers – each sprouting a 4 in long claw - on each hand. This grotesque animal, or apparition, first introduced itself to humanity around 2 a.m. on 29 June 1988, near Scape Ore Swamp, outside the one-horse town of Bishopville in Lee County, South Carolina.

Seventeen-year-old Christopher Davis had just finished changing a flat tyre on his car when he saw 'something large' running towards him across a nearby field. As the creature came nearer, Davis leaped into the vehicle and tried to slam the door – only to see the thing seize it and try to wrench it open. Davis had plenty of time – more than he would have liked – to note the fine details of its unlovely appearance. Davis eventually got the car going and made his getaway. When he got home, shaking with fright, he found long scratches on the car roof, and the wing mirror in serious disarray.

Just three months after Davis had seen the Lizard Man, Kenneth Orr, an airman stationed at Shaw Air Force Base in South Carolina, filed a police report saying that he had also encountered a strange reptilian creature while driving down Highway 15. He claimed to have shot and wounded the creature. In evidence he presented several scales and a sample of the creature's blood for analysis. However, two days later he was arrested for unlawfully carrying a gun and he recanted his story. He told the police that he had invented the sighting in an effort to keep the stories of Lizard Man alive.

Others encountered Lizard Man that summer, but none helped solve the mystery of what the creature was. However, records show that scaly and apparently aquatic man-beasts have been reported before, in many parts of North America.

Such creatures sound like a fantasy, or a hoax, or merely the effect on surprised witnesses of a person in a diving suit. But there is an odd twist to the Lizard Man tale, especially if one bears in mind the possibility that bigfoot and its international relations may be a surviving form of the officially extinct Gigantopithecus. In 1982, palaeontologists Drs Dale A. Russell and R. Skguin of the Canadian National Museum of Natural Sciences published a paper in which they set out what a dinosaurian equivalent of a human being may have looked like, had the dinosaurs survived to the present. They suggest it would have been a two-legged creature with three-fingered hands, and in general would have looked startlingly like Lizard Man.

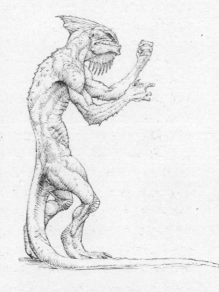

An artist's impression of Lizard Man.

MONSTERS FROM THE DEEP

Since pre-biblical times, sailors have returned home from long voyages with tales of huge monsters and cunning sea serpents. Many stories can be attributed to the lonely nights at sea, and alcoholic solace, but should these include the testimony of senior naval officers, and the unidentifiable carcasses washed up upon remote shores?

'He had a large body and a small alligator-like head. The neck seemed to be medium size, matching the size of the head. The body was very large, shaped somewhat like a seal. There was a mane of bristly hair or fur which ran down the middle of his head.

'He would surface the upper part of his body and glide out of the water with the lower part of his body remaining submerged. The portion of his body which was visible measured about 40 feet in length. We estimate his weight to be between 35 and 40 tons over all.

'At no time did the whole body show. He stayed on the surface no longer than 40 seconds at a time. You could hear the heavy weight of his upper body when he dove below, creating a large splash and a subsequent wake. He surfaced four times in 20 minutes during which we were trying to stay clear of him. The Captain changed course to steer away from him and the queer fellow surfaced on our starboard beam...

'Another peculiar thing about him was that when he'd surface he would turn his head looking towards us and it seemed to us he was playful and curious. Another point was that on the upper part of his body there were two flippers, similar to those of a seal.'

So runs part of a report of a sea-monster sighting on 3 September 1959 by the cook, Joseph H. Bourassa, of the scalloper *Noreen*. The ship was 120 miles out from Bermuda, east of Pollock. Bourassa had been at sea for 20 years, and had never before seen anything like what he saw that day.

NAVAL REPORTS

What are sea monsters? How many kinds of them are there? Compare Bourassa's account with this, from an officer of the Imperial German Navy who was aboard the U-boat U28 when, during World War One, the submarine blew the British Iberian out of the water in the North Atlantic:

'A little later pieces of wreckage, and among them a gigantic sea-animal, writhing and struggling wildly, were shot out of the water to a height of 60 to 100 feet... the animal sank out of sight after 10 or 15 seconds... It was about 60 feet long, was like a crocodile in shape and had four limbs with powerful webbed feet and a long tail tapering to a point.'

If this creature bears little enough resemblance to the animal in the first account quoted, try this one:

'Then I saw this great eel-like monster rear its head like a Scotch terrier struck by curiosity. Its eyes were red and green, like the port and starboard lights of a ship. It was about ninety feet long. As we approached within 200 feet, it rose out of the water, with its seven humps like a camel and its face like a cow, and didn't make any noise, but I thought it should have mooed. Then it uttered an eerie bellow, like a bull whale in its last agony and reared up, perhaps thirty feet, perhaps fifty, and flopped over on its back. Along its flanks was a phosphorescent glow. By this time we had five searchlights on it, and it turned to the side and dived.'

The report came from First Officer A.E. Richards, who witnessed the episode from the bridge of the liner *Santa Lucia* in the long thin dawn light of 21 October 1933. The ship was off Sheringham Point near Victoria, in Cadboro Bay, Vancouver Island, British Columbia. The bay is famous for its resident sea monster 'Caddy' or, more pretentiously, Cadborosaurus.

One more example will drive home the point to which we are making so laborious a pilgrimage:

'It looked like an elephant waving its trunk, but the trunk was a long neck with a small head on the end, like a snake's head. It had humps on the back which moved in a funny way. The colour was black or very dark brown, and the skin seemed to be like a sealion's... the animal frightened me... I do not like the way it moved when it was swimming.'

'The animal' is called morgawr, the Cornish Celtic word for 'sea giant'. It made many appearances off the Cornish coast in the 1970s, and this particular witness, known only as Mary R, actually managed to photograph it, in February 1976, as it played in the sea off Rosemullion Head near Falmouth. The creature bears a striking resemblance to the popular image of the Loch Ness monster, and for all anyone knows may be of the same family, although Mary F. estimated its length to be no more than 15–18 ft – a veritable infant beside Nessie, and a positive midget compared to the monstrous 'eel-like' animal that First Officer Richards saw disporting itself off Vancouver Island.

PANDORA'S BOX

A German U-boat of World War One vintage. When one such craft torpedoed a British freighter, a 60 ft long sea serpent was blown out of the water at the same time.

And there lies the rub. On the face of it, no one sea monster seems to bear much likeness to another. So what are we dealing with? The usual catalogue of possibilities and explanations presents itself unbidden – hallucinations, mis-identifications, bored sailors livening up a ship's log to bemuse posterity, tired and emotional witnesses (considerably less of a rarity at sea than monster sightings: many long-haul freighters are navigated through a sea-fog of alcohol).

Or are we back in the world of officially extinct or simply officially overlooked animals? There is some reason to believe that some apparently extinct creatures have survived in the sea. The ostensibly freshwater Loch Ness monster, for instance, may be a marine animal, a surviving plesiosaur, that merely visits the Loch on occasion. On the evidence, there is no compelling reason to suppose for an instant that scientists have catalogued all the animals that live in the world's oceans. The waters, after all, cover roughly two-thirds of the surface of the Earth, and they keep on presenting little surprises to our friends in the laboratory coats. Just to cite three examples: in 1958, a previously unknown species of porpoise, now called the 'cochito', was found in the Gulf of California; eight years later 'megamouth' was discovered, hauled up on the anchor of a Hawaiian survey ship – a shark so different from other sharks that zoologists had to create an entire new family to accommodate it, and it duly entered the record books, too, as the third largest known species of its kind; and in 1983 a new species of killer whale, the Prudes Bay, peculiar to the Antarctic, was added to zoology's roll of honour.

Honest scientists know that they have not plumbed the depths of the riches of life hidden in the oceans. The same honesty makes their hair, quite rightly, stand on end at the thought that untold biological riches are being destroyed in the Amazon rainforests every day. Biologists do not know what

A massive sea serpent was spotted from HMS Daedalus *in 1848, and this engraving was based on an eyewitnesses's drawing sent to the Lords of the Admiralty by Captain M'Quhoe, the ship's commander.*

we may be losing as the fires of greed consume trees, herbs, insects, mammals and birds by the square mile every minute. They only know such a vast and fecund area must be a living treasure house. So it is with the seas of the world. There have to be creatures there waiting, willingly or not, to be discovered, but the seas of the world are harder, vaster, more expansive and more treacherous to explore than any rainforest, and that is the scientists' problem.

MONSTERS OF THE BIBLICAL SEAS

Our problem, for the time being – perhaps in the forlorn hope of persuading scientists to recognize that there is a potentially fruitful field of research waiting to be taken up – is to make sense of such material as we have. There is plenty of circumstantial evidence that sea monsters exist: but how good is it? Leaving aside the mistakes, hallucinations, hoaxes and misperceptions of drunken sailors, we are left with two basic possibilities as to the origin or reality of sea monsters.

First is the possibility that some, at least, of the reported sightings are of animals that have survived their official 'extinction'. Second is the possibility that these are creatures – some rare, some perhaps less so – that have simply eluded the eyes of science. They are not 'unknown' or 'unexplained' animals, but simply unidentified ones.

Whatever we are dealing with, there is nothing new about them. Large and terrifying animals have been known to exist since Old Testament times, and from the days before those ancient texts were written as well. Jonah was swallowed by a 'whale'. The other monster of the biblical seas, Leviathan, is also mentioned in greater or lesser detail in various places in the Psalms of David, and the Books of Isaiah and Job. One senses that these passages reveal what only the Lord can know of creatures that swim beneath the face of the deep.

'HUGEST OF LIVING CREATURES'

The most extensive description of Leviathan comes in Chapter 41 of that dark, bejewelled hymn to an ancient existentialism, the Book of Job. In this, the Lord continues to upbraid Job for his presumptions, and paints a picture of such power that one cannot help feeling not only that the passage seems to be celebrating the tremendous vitality of this creature, but that it is revered even by the one that created it:

'Canst thou draw out leviathan with an hook? or his tongue with a cord which thou lettest down?

Wilt thou play with him as with a bird? or wilt thou bind him for thy maidens?

Shall the companions make a banquet of him? shall they part him among the merchants?

Lay thine hand upon him, remember the battle, do no more.

Behold, the hope of him is in vain; shall not one be cast down even at the sight of him?

None is so fierce that dare stir him up ...

Who can open the doors of his face? his teeth are terrible round about.

His scales are his pride, shut up together as with a close seal.

The flakes of his flesh are joined together: they are firm in themselves; they cannot be moved.

When he raiseth himself up, the mighty are afraid: by reason of breakings they purify themselves.

He esteemeth iron as straw, and brass as rotten wood.

The arrow cannot make him flee: sling-stones are turned with him into stubble.

He maketh the deep to boil like a pot: he maketh the sea like a pot of ointment.

He maketh a path to shine after him; one would think the deep to be hoary.

Upon earth there is not his like, who is made without fear.

He beholdeth all high things: he is a king over all the children of pride.'

All the elements of a sea-monster sighting seem to be here: the terrific size, the sense of its enormous strength and invulnerability, the confident – even casual – indifference of the creature to its puny human observers, and its sheer, awe-inspiring strangeness.

A 17th-century English poet, John Milton, a mere bricklayer in comparison to the Hebrew architect of language, was also entranced by this creature, but he could only grope blindly to recapture the drift of his predecessor's magnificent vision:

'There Leviathan Hugest of living creatures, on the deep
Stretch'd like a promontory sleeps or swims,
And seems a moving land . . .'

But what was Leviathan? Can we tell, at this distance in time?

A TWISTED SERPENT

The translators of the Anglican Church's Authorised Version of the Bible appointed by King James did not actually translate the original Hebrew word, which was livyathun, probably because they could not connect its meaning to anything they knew in their own world. Literally, it means 'twisted serpent'.

The 5th- or 6th-century BC Jewish poet who recorded the trials of Job seems himself to have had only a sketchy idea of what Leviathan was. The ancient Hebrews, curiously, were not a seafaring nation, although they were always within reach of the Mediterranean Sea. Possibly all sea beasts were somewhat mysterious to them, although they would have been aware that some were of unnaturally large size.

The vision of a monstrous sea animal that possessed the poet who wrote the Book of Job was possibly, and in part, derived from sightings of whales or sharks. The most likely source was probably foreign sailors' accounts of sperm whales, the animals on which the neighbouring Phoenicians – known in the Bible as Canaanites, and living in what is now

Lebanon – based their whaling industry.

The biblical story of Job is based on a Middle Eastern (not Hebrew) legend much older than the poet who re-created it, and his notion of Leviathan was almost certainly influenced by regional tales of dragons. Images of monsters mentioned in the myths of Egypt or Assyria, such as Tiamat and Apophis, would also have influenced the poet's vision. 'Leviathan', then, means any great sea or land monster.

The Belgian zoologist Dr Bernard Heuvelmans, who has made the most detailed study of sea-monster reports in modern times, suggests that Chapter 41 of Job, quoted in part above, suggests not the whale but a melodramatic account of a long-necked sea serpent.

The phrases describing a creature that 'raiseth himself' up out of the water and 'beholdeth all high things' certainly suggest an animal with a long neck. And 'the flakes of his flesh [translated elsewhere as 'the members of his body'] are joined together' may be a half-explanatory reference to the sinuous humped appearance of these creatures that (now as then) so many modern reports of sea monsters also mention.

This aspect of Leviathan rather qualifies the possibility that the true source of its reputation is the sperm whale or sharks. This is also the moment to remark on the sceptics' claim that the 'humps' of sea monsters are really a misperception of dolphins leaping in line. This is the kind of dozy (and pretty desperate) rationalization that could only come from people who have never seen dolphins in the sea. They are unmistakable for anything but dolphins.

Was Leviathan no more than a compound of mythical beasts, hearsay, and ignorance? Or was it all that, but with the hearsay relating directly to actual sea monsters? This seems at least possible. Leviathan, then, is at least partly a genuine unidentified creature.

BEEF-RED FLESH

In June 1983, amateur naturalist Owen Burnham was on holiday with his family on the coast of the Gambia, West Africa, taking a break from their home in neighbouring Senegal. During the night of 11/12 June, a large unidentified animal was washed ashore on the beach near where they were staying. They heard about this the following morning. At 8.30 a.m. Burnham, together with his brother and sister and father, went down to the shore to look for the creature. They found it easily enough, along with two Africans who were trying to sever its head so that they could sell the skull to tourists.

The animal was battered, distended with internal gas, and smelled foul, but it was essentially complete and had not begun to decompose. It had not been dead long. Burnham was familiar with all of the major land and sea creatures native to the region, but he was unable to identify this one. The group persuaded the two native entrepreneurs to stop for long enough to let them measure the animal. Burnham, lacking a camera, also made sketches of it and counted the teeth.

The animal was smooth-skinned, with four flippers. One hind flipper had been torn off, and the other damaged. Its overall length was about 15 ft, of which 5 ft were taken up by a long, pointed tail whose cross-section was like a rounded-off triangle. The animal had a slightly domed forehead, and at the end of its 18 in long snout were what looked like a pair of nostrils. Thinking it might be some form of marine mammal (a whale or dolphin), Burnham looked for a blowhole, but found none. Nor could he see any mammary glands. If there were any male organs they were too damaged to recognize. The creature's long, thin jaws were very tightly closed; Burnham said he had 'a job' to prise them apart. He counted 80 teeth, which he noted were evenly distributed, very sharp, and

The alleged sea monster photographed by Robert Le Serrec at Stonehaven Bay, Hook Island, Australia, on 12 December 1964.

similar in shape to a barracuda's but whiter and thicker.

The flippers were round and solid. There were no toes, claws or nails. When the Africans returned and completed their work of removing the head, the witnesses could see that the animal's vertebrae were very thick. It took the men 20 minutes' dedicated hacking with a machete to sever it. The animal's flesh was dark red, 'like beef'.

Burnham speaks Mandinka, the local language, fluently and asked the men the name of the animal. They told him kunthum belein, Mandinka for 'cutting jaws'; this is what the coastal fishermen call dolphins.

Burnham later described the unknown animal to many native fishermen in the area in the hope that they might be able to identify it, but none had ever seen anything like it. He concluded that the butchers on the beach had called it a 'dolphin' because it looked vaguely like one.

Burnham then wrote to various authorities on wildlife to try to get further leads, but got no real help. Most suggested animals that he had already been able to rule out thanks to his familiarity with the denizens of the region. Burnham also said that he 'looked through encyclopedias and every book I could lay hands on' in trying to identify the mystery animal. Eventually, he found a photograph of the skull of the extinct Australian *Kronosaurus queenslandicus*, which he felt was the nearest thing he had seen so far. However, he noted that that skull was 10 ft long: clearly it was not the same as the creature he had seen.

AWESOME

Burnham's detailed reports of his find, and the sketches and measurements he made, were analysed at length by zoologist Dr Karl Shuker in the mid-1980s. Shuker rapidly ruled out a number of near-contenders, and realized that the only creatures that at all resembled Burnham's find had long since died out – and, what was more, had been extinct for more than 60 million years. One was the pliosaur, a family of short-necked plesiosaurs that included the Kronosaurus whose skull Burnham had recognized but rejected. The other was a group of non-scaly sea crocodiles, called thalattosuchians, who had slender bodies and four paddle-like limbs. Their tails had a dorsal fin, but a thalattosuchian whose fin had been torn off or scuffed away would look amazingly like the beast of Burnham's sketches. And if thalattosuchians had survived into the present, it is possible that they would no longer have such a fin.

Without any physical remains for direct examination, however, the Gambian creature cannot be positively identified one way or the other. But the Gambian find suggests, at least, that not all of the reptiles of prehistory died out with the dinosaurs.

Burnham himself says: 'When I think of the coelacanth I don't like to think what could be at the bottom of the sea. I'm not looking for a prehistoric animal, only trying to identify what was the strangest thing I'll ever see. I couldn't believe this creature was lying in front of me. Even now I can remember every minute detail of it. To see such a thing was awesome.'

ESCAPING DETECTION

The magnum opus of sea-monster studies is Belgian cryptozoologist Dr Bernard Heuvelmans's *In the Wake of the Sea Serpents*. In this, Heuvelmans analysed 587 sea-monster sightings made between 1639 and 1964. After disposing of hoaxes, misidentifications and reports too vague to be useful, he was still left with 358 sightings, and was able to sort these into nine basic types.

These are the 'long necked' sea serpent – the most often-reported of all sea monsters, with four flippers, a cigar-shaped body and a capacity for swimming very fast indeed – which grows to between 15 and 65 ft long; marine saurians, seen only in tropical waters in mid-ocean, which may reach 60 ft in length; merhorses; many-humped monsters; super-otters (not reported since 1848 and possibly now extinct); many-finned monsters; super-eels; fathers-of-all-the-turtles; and yellow-bellies. The last Heuvelmans believes may be an as yet unidentified fish, possibly a shark.

THALASSOMEDON

This specimen of the extinct marine reptile, Thalassomedon, was discovered in 1939 in the Graneros Shale of Caca County, Colorado and is now on display in the Denver Museum of Nature and Science.

The Thalassomedon (meaning 'Lord of the Seas') was a giant sea reptile from the Mesozoic era, that lived in the open seas and breathed air. It was a real life sea monster from approximately 95 million years ago. It lived in the inland sea that originally covered the majority of the western part of North America, and was a member of the Elasmosauridae family. It was known to reach 40 feet (12 m) in length, and the skull was close to 18.7 inches (47 cm). It had a long snout, teeth that could be anything up to 1.9 inches (5 cm) long and an incredibly long neck of about 20 feet (6 m). The Thalassomedon had 63 vertebrae, four flippers and a reasonably short tail.

These marine reptiles were air breathers that had to return to the surface periodically or else drown, like modern whales and dolphins, and most species seemed to have preferred shallow waters rather than deep ocean. Relatives of these sea creatures still exist today and could easily be mistaken for monsters of the deep.

On that basis there is no logical reason why the seas should not be hiding any number of unidentified species of animal (especially if they are both shy and few in number) from the official catalogues of marine science. They will doubtless continue to roam the oceans, bemuse and astonish those few who are lucky enough to spot them, and be overlooked by the guardians of orthodoxy. Probably the creatures themselves would prefer it to stay that way.

PAGAN PLACE, PAGAN POWERS

The ancient remains of powerful pagan civilizations cast long shadows into the present. The bright light of scientific investigation only deepens the mysteries surrounding the strange occurrences and unnerving experiences, and makes the shadows darker still…

While the Earth is full of strange, unexpected and inexplicable creatures, it is no less replete with mysterious and enigmatic works of mankind itself.

The ancient remains of lost civilizations – the great monuments of Stonehenge in England, Carnac in France, the Serpent Mound in Ohio, USA, the stone circles of West Africa – are only the most renowned of a myriad of such sites whose purpose is still obscure and whose meaning has been all but lost with the passing of those who built them.

Yet the world's mysterious places exercise a perennial fascination. They do so not simply because we still do not really understand them, or because they are awesome in themselves; but partly, at least, because we sense that they were enigmatic even to the people who created them.

Very strange things are traditionally said to happen at ancient sites. Very strange things still happen in such places today.

THE PETRIFIED MAIDENS

According to the pioneeering 'Earth mysteries' researcher Paul Devereux, a number of people have had bizarre experiences while passing along a particular 300 yd long stretch of a country lane that runs past the ancient stone circle called Rollright in Oxfordshire, England. One, a member of the Dragon Project research group, was watching a car containing two people approach the stone circle along the road – when the vehicle vanished. On another occasion, a scientist saw a huge, dog-like creature with coarse grey hair momentarily appear and then vanish. Another witness, a woman, saw an old-fashioned gypsy caravan briefly appear and then disappear in much the same way.

Odd occurrences have been associated with such megalithic sites since time immemorial, and the stones, then as now, have been held to possess mysterious powers. There is nothing new about stone circles attracting, or generating, spectres, visions of fairies and other odd creatures from folklore such as black dogs (an instance of which was, presumably, what was seen by the scientist noted above). At the Bryn-yr-Ellyllon mound near Mold in Wales, for example, a huge golden figure has been seen on many occasions – and the name of the barrow itself means 'hill of the goblins'.

It is commonly believed that the number of individual stones in certain circles cannot be counted, although many sites are associated with specific numbers, most often the key mystical figures of three, seven and nine. Possibly one reason they cannot be counted is that, so the legends say, they can move of their own accord. Many stones are reputed to resist any attempt to move them but, if they are shifted out of place by some means, will put themselves back where they came from. Others are still more independent. One such is the Enstone near Oxford – it is particularly regular in its habits: it reputedly takes a drink every midnight at a neighbouring stream.

There may be a connection between this kind of belief and the tradition that many standing stones, especially groups of them, were once people, now petrified. The Merry Maidens in Cornwall are so called because that is what they once were – a mite too merry, perhaps, as they danced themselves to exhaustion and turned to stone where they collapsed. Nearby are the musicians, presumably responsible for whipping them into their frenzy: the Two Pipers, and the Blind Fiddler, now pillars of granite. The Rollright Stones are reputedly a king and his knights, petrified by a witch.

Not all the powers associated with the ancient stones are so spooky: many have the reputation of being able to heal or impart healing properties. Water that has been splashed on the stones at Stonehenge will cure ailments. Sick children were traditionally passed through the hole in the famous Men-an-Tol in Cornwall. Other sites have the same capacity, especially those associated with water such as holy wells and ancient spas. There is evidence that the baths at Bath, for instance, have been regarded as curative for some 7,000 years.

All these unexpected properties have one thing in common: they suggest that there is something strangely alive about these places. They are, in other words, places where a peculiar kind of energy concentrates. This half-hidden idea is reflected in another tradition about ancient places – that many of them are associated with dragons. Stories, myths and legends occur in virtually all cultures, all over the world, of a serpent, worm or dragon whose qualities are, to say the least, peculiarly ambiguous. So it is worth taking a brief survey of dragon-lore before pondering how it fits into the puzzle of the ancient sites.

The Rollright Stones in Oxfordshire, which have been known to exert very peculiar influences on people in their vicinity.

THE DRAGON GUARDS

In the oldest Indian and Babylonian myths, which are roughly 4,000 years old, the destruction of an enraged dragon brings the release of life-giving waters. These myths are not moral fables, but creation myths – poetic accounts of how the world was made. The importance of the dragon in these stories is that it releases an indispensable source of life and energy into the world – but at the price of having to confront the creature.

Everyone familiar with Genesis is aware of the double nature of the serpent in the Garden of Eden. It is an actual, physical presence, and also it represents a singular moral dilemma. To follow the path of the serpent, as Adam and Eve do, is to lose paradise and innocence but to gain knowledge and moral responsibility – free will.

This theme runs through all serpent myths, all over the world. In Anglo-Saxon Britain, the epic – and essentially pagan – poem *Beowulf* revolves in part around a fire-breathing 'worm' – in other words, a dragon – who is enraged because one of the aging Beowulf's subjects has stolen a cup from the hoard of treasure it has guarded for three centuries. (The poet makes a point of saying that dragons seek out and hoard treasure.) In killing the dragon, Beowulf is mortally wounded. Once again, the serpent is associated with something desirable and yet destructive. His power is also, finally, irresistible, and is potent in the cause of both good and ill.

Anglo-Saxon culture, like any other, had many roots. What we see in *Beowulf* is the fruit of tendrils that reach back to Norse and Celtic mythology, and beyond that to legends that have their known beginnings thousands of years ago, in the mythology of the Indo-European peoples of Central Asia. From the point of view of an investigation of prehistoric sites, what is also significant in this European dragon tradition is its

Circular, holed stones like this one at Men-an-Tol, Cornwall, are reputed to have mysterious powers of healing.

connection with another piece of lore about the sites themselves: that is that many of them are reputed to be built on hoards of buried treasure.

The golden spectre seen at Bryn-yr-Ellyllon may be a reflection of this folk memory. Like the stones themselves, some hoards have minds of their own. At the neolithic mound of Willy Howe in north-eastern England, there is a tale that local people once attempted to dig out the chest of gold concealed at its centre. They tried to drag it from the earth with horses, but the chest simply burrowed deeper into the ground. As might be expected, many such prehistoric hoards are said to be guarded by dragons. Attempts at finding its secrets in 1857 and again 30 years later, yielded nothing except a pit which was about 9 feet (2.7 m) deep.

TREACHEROUS ELEMENTS

It's clear that in Western and Middle Eastern dragon-lore, the creature has both a material and a spiritual energy, but it is one that is neither simple nor entirely trustworthy.

Take the paradox that these fiery creatures have an affinity for water, for example. Water is the most treacherous element as well as the most vital. The same may be said of fire, the other 'element' that is inseparable from any concept of dragons. One hidden lesson here seems to be that both the most basic materials of survival and the great abstractions like moral freedom have a potential for both good and evil. Another hidden message is that struggle is inherent in all our dealings with the contradictory forces of life, despite the fact that we depend on them – or perhaps because we depend on them.

The most fundamental lesson that underlies these perceptions is that these are eternal verities; they are the very basic stuff of life. And so the spirit of the dragon never entirely dies. Indeed, in the Babylonian myth, the dragon was also the mother of all living things and, despite being slain, continues her immortal existence as a monstrous serpent who makes herself visible in wild storms at sea.

Dragons are everywhere associated with the most fundamental aspects of life. In the Mayan culture of Central America, which flourished between about AD 150 and AD 900, the serpent was 'lord of fire and time', and was also responsible for causing floods, earthquakes and storms. It is strange, given the distance between the Americas and Asia, that Chinese dragons are so similar in this respect.

In China, a vast and intricate dragon-lore grew up that detailed not only how long a dragon might live (5,000 years) and how many scales it had (81 or 117, depending on the school of thought) but the medicinal virtues of its teeth, liver or saliva and the significance of its behaviour as an augury of the weather.

Chinese dragons are, by Western standards, quite benevolent, but they too have an ambiguous nature. They are capable of shape-shifting, appearing in the guise of familiar animals at will, and, most importantly, they control the weather – which, as everyone knows, is neither predictable nor always benign. And to this day the Chinese believe that their dragons must be appeased and placated. The art of feng shui, which means 'wind and water', is entirely devoted to avoiding any disturbance to the 'paths of the dragon' (lung mei) when siting buildings in the landscape. Expert geomancers – 'earth diviners' – make elaborate calculations to ensure that this balance of nature Is maintained. A famous modern example of their work is the alignment of the Hong Kong and Shanghai Bank in Hong Kong.

One of the most baffling and yet fascinating of all the enigmas associated with prehistoric sites and 'Earth mysteries' studies is the universal nature of dragon-lore. That the same image should reflect so many similar intuitions in so many different cultures, separated by huge gulfs of time and geography, suggests that we are confronted by something absolutely fundamental in the human psyche. And more; that this in turn suggests that the human mind has grasped something crucial about the nature of the Earth itself.

We have, in the dragon, an extraordinary concentration of ideas: a mythical beast that guards material or spiritual riches; the energies of the elements; and a connection with sites of 'Earth energy'. Researchers have also established that there is a connection between the ancient sites, the so-called ley lines that often connect them, and UFO sightings. Is it possible that dragons and UFOs are different forms of the same 'Earth energy'? And if so, are they shaped by the mind into the form most suited to a particular epoch – or do they cause the mind to perceive them in the most acceptable way?

That there are energies in the Earth, that they are most powerful around prehistoric sites, and that they have real effects on human consciousness, is attested not only by the feng shui geomancers and the long traditions of folklore – but by modern reports too.

WEIRD SENSATIONS

Paul Devereux collected one such account from local government official Peter Thornborrow. He was walking through the stone circle called Long Meg and Her Daughters in Cumbria, when he was suddenly assailed by a bizarre sensation of dizziness. He felt, he said later, as if he was 'not really there... not really in the same time'. He leaned against one of the stones to recover his normal senses. It responded by giving him what he could only describe as 'an electric shock'.

Devereux has also recorded that in 1986, as a young couple were driving on a country lane beside Cam Ingli, a peak and sacred site in the Preseli Hills in Pembrokeshire, west Wales, the girl felt a weird sensation of physical discomfort. She was sure the feeling was caused by the peak. The pair decided to test the idea. They drove on until the girl felt normal again, and then turned the car around and drove back over the same route. Once again, as they neared Carn Ingli, the strange and uncomfortable sensation returned.

Modern experience and traditional lore thus combine to confirm the strangeness of prehistoric sites. There is a long-standing belief that experiences like the two recounted above and the legacy of folklore clinging to these ancient places indicate that some form of paranormal or psychic energy is at work in them. Since the turn of the century, psychics have attempted to pick up the local 'vibrations' at standing stones, circles, barrows and mounds, and since the 1930s dowsers too have tried to unravel the secrets of these places. Unfortunately, the claimed results and 'discoveries' at any one site have been as many and various as the number of psychics or dowsers who have tried their skills there.

The aptly named Dragon Project was launched in England in 1977 to bring a comprehensive set of research methods to bear on the question of what kinds of energies might be present at prehistoric sites. The project was launched in 1977 and a group of volunteers from various disciplines, conducted many years of physical monitoring at sites in the United Kingdom and other countries. The project decided to pursue two parallel lines of investigation: there would be room for dowsers and psychics to follow their own form of detective work, while a variety of scientific detection instruments would be used to search out and record the more conventional physical attributes of the sites.

This has involved recording levels of magnetism, radio-activity, infra-red radiation, among known physical forces, as well as recording and studying unexplained but theoretically conventional effects such as the strange light phenomena that have long been reported at or near many ancient sites. The psychic side of the research has been as inconclusive as any of the other attempts to use mind power to probe the secrets of the ancients, but the second, scientific line of enquiry has thrown up some intriguing results. Although this kind of monitoring deals in the standard scientific measures of physics, the actual levels discovered at the sites have been by no means conventional or consistent with normal, average ('background') levels for the areas concerned.

Science has begun to confirm folklore.

SECRET KNOWLEDGE – SECRET PURPOSES

At Long Meg, where Peter Thornborrow had the bizarre experience described earlier, Dragon Project researchers found that several of the standing stones there had small patches on them that were emitting a constant stream of gamma rays – in short, they were radioactive. The stones concerned were granite, which is naturally radioactive, but not to the degree of these particular stones. And it is distinctly unusual for granite to emit radiation of any kind from concentrated energy points such as these stones possessed.

Dragons might be defeated by the most irreverent means, but gaining the treasure of knowledge in their keeping would always bring fresh challenges.

This may or may not have been responsible for Thornborrow's experience, but researchers have noted that in places where natural radiation – from granite or other radioactive minerals, or from radon gas seeping from the ground – is higher than normal, some people have experienced apparently altered states of consciousness. Monitoring the radiation levels around the Rollright Stones revealed a fascinating fact about the 300 yd stretch of country lane where at least three people – whose accounts we gave above – had reported seeing spectral visions. Geiger counters showed far higher than normal background readings of radiation here.

Its source, the researchers concluded, was probably in energetic rocks in the hardcore used to lay the road's foundations. This, like the stones at the ancient site, had come from local quarries – which suggests that whoever put the Rollright Stones in place was aware that the local rock had very special qualities. Those qualities were interesting to them because they serve their purposes. The key question after that is: what were their purposes? Some other odd qualities of ancient sites may help to get us nearer the answer to this crucial question.

RADIOACTIVE BURIAL CHAMBERS

People have experienced different strange effects at other sites with greater than the usual 'background' natural radiation. At Boleigh Fogou, an Iron Age underground stone chamber or 'souterrain' built from granite in Cornwall, a psychologist saw mysterious swirls and points of light moving over the inner rock surfaces. Similarly, inside the 5,000-year-old Cornish dolmen called Chun Quoit, archaeologist John Barnatt and photographer Brian Larkman both saw bands of light flashing along the underside of the capstone.

Boleigh Fogou – A fogou is an archaeological hole in the ground dating from between about 500 BCE to 500 CE. This means that they really are Celtic, unlike the older standing stones and stone circles.

Most of Europe's ancient underground chambers of this kind are in areas whose basic rock formations are of granite, or where uranium has been found, so it can hardly be insignificant that in North America, Pueblo Indian underground ritual chambers, known as 'kivas', were likewise built in uranium-rich areas of what are now the Southwestern States. Bearing that in mind, it comes as no surprise to learn that the King's Chamber in Egypt's Great Pyramid was specially clad in granite, and that when members of the Dragon Project monitored the King's Chamber they found enhanced radiation levels there, at levels at least as high as those found inside the granite monuments of Britain.

The great stone sites of the ancient world are not unique among ancient monuments in registering unusually high – although by no means dangerous – levels of nuclear radiation. Holy wells, too, can be mildly radioactive, and there is evidence to suggest that at such 'homeopathic' levels nuclear radiation is actually beneficial, not harmful. As mentioned earlier, the famous hot springs at Bath, England have been known as healing waters for some 70 centuries, and are mildly radio-active. The waters of Chalice Well, Glastonbury – one of the holiest places in the world, if the legends are to be believed – are said to be radioactive. Dragon Project researchers have also recorded higher-than-average readings from geiger counters at a number of holy wells in the Celtic fringes of Britain in Wales, Cornwall and Scotland.

MAGNETIC MAGIC

Ancient sites, stone circles and solitary standing stones have all been known for decades to have strange effects on compasses and lodestones. Go to a standing stone or similar ancient site and the chances are it is in a place where there are peculiarities in the Earth's local magnetic field, or that it throws the standard measuring equipment – the gaussometer – out of true by a marked margin.

The Dragon Project found that scattered about Carn Ingli were areas where there were powerful anomalies in the local magnetic field. In these places, compass needles point south instead of north, and gaussometers show unexpected readings. As for individual stones creating bizarre magnetic effects – or being carefully placed where those effects are most marked – there is a host of instances. At Castlerigg, Cumbria, only the westernmost stone, alone among 38 stones at the circle, affects a compass needle. At the Gors Fawr stone circle in Wales, the outlying pillar, which indicates the direction of the midsummer sunrise, is also the only magnetic

Stonehenge, the most elaborately built of all the ancient megalithic sites.

stone at the site. A serpentine outcrop on Mount Tamalpais, San Francisco (a magical place for the local American Indians), similarly causes compasses to spin. There are many other examples, and they can be found all over the world.

Even stranger is another magnetic anomaly that Dragon Project researchers have found at many ancient sites. They discovered that some standing stones show sudden fluctuations in their magnetic fields that last for only a few hours. Similar effects were found, quite independently of the Dragon Project work, at the Rollright Circle by the retired engineer Charles Brooker, who reported his discoveries in the international journal *New Scientist* in 1983.

The nature of these short-lived magnetic pulses is not understood by modern science, so what significance they may have had for the ancients so many thousands of years ago must be today entirely a matter for speculation. But then so is the means whereby the peoples of the ancient world, lacking modern instrumentation, recognized these qualities in the sites and in the stones they chose, in the first place. And why they chose them for these qualities is another question altogether.

THE STONES ARE SINGING

Some of the unexplained phenomena at ancient sites would not have needed any exotic instruments to detect. One is the often-reported appearance of peculiar and apparently intelligent lights in, around or near prehistoric remains. Another is the persistent presence of inexplicable noises at these places.

While alone inside Stonehenge one early morning in 1983, Gabriele Wilson heard a 'ringing' sound from one of the stones. At midsummer in 1987, Michael Woolf and Rachel Garcia heard 'a sudden, muffled thunderclap' that seemed to come 'from beneath the earth' at the 11 ft tall Blind Fiddler stone in Cornwall. Other researchers at the Rollright Stones have reported curious clicking noises issuing from the ground at night.

The ancients themselves witnessed such odd sounds at their sacred sites, as well. The two 60 ft tall statues known as the Colossi of Memnon, in the Valley of the Kings in Egypt, were cracked during an earthquake in 27 BC. After that, the northernmost of the two statues began to emit a strange sound at dawn each day. The noise was variously described as 'soft' and 'bell-like', 'a musical note' and even (by contrast) like 'a cord snapping'. People flocked from far and wide to the massive statue in the belief that it would act as an oracle. The sounds stopped when the cracks were eventually repaired.

Whatever the cause of these particular noises, modern researchers have long known that sounds at extremely high 'ultrasound' frequencies – well beyond the range of normal human hearing – can be detected at dawn coming from standing stones.

In January 1987 Dragon Project workers discovered that a 3 ft band around the middle of the tallest stone at the Rollright Circle was the source of a signal being picked up by their ultrasound receiver. The signal always ebbed away as the day wore on. It is possible that these signals were the by-product of transmissions from nearby military telecommunications stations, resonating in crystals in the stones. There is nothing secret or occult in the fact that crystals are sensitive to radio waves. On the other hand, the effect could be caused by some unknown process occurring in the Earth itself.

CENTRES OF POWER

The folklore interpretation of the weird sounds and lights that have been heard and seen around ancient sites has been quite logical, but it has also probably been back-to-front.

People who have intuitively recognized something strange about the ancient places have attributed other signs of their uniqueness to the spirits, ghosts or even fairies to whom they feel these places belong. But almost certainly this view is the wrong way round. It is much more likely that the sites for stone circles, burial mounds, kivas and other ceremonial centres were chosen exactly because they were (in the eyes of the builders, those who saw them first) already magical. Throwing out strange noises and weird darting lights, such sites were advertising themselves as ideal for magical purposes.

As we have seen, these signs were also signals – that even stranger effects would take place in these places on the minds of those brave enough to enter them. How those effects were taken advantage of and controlled is one of the central mysteries of the purpose of the prehistoric sites.

This mystery may not be entirely unsolved, but even to glimpse the solution, we must first look at the stars, the Sun and the Moon, the tree at the centre of the world, and at mysterious patterns on a parched desert floor.

CELESTIAL SIGNS IN SACRED PLACES

Stonehenge, with its toppled stones and sad grandeur, is but the last in a series of sacred temples which changed drastically in both appearance and purpose over several thousand years. The original Stonehenge was a place of earth and timber – and rotting corpses.

The curious physical qualities of the sites where the ancients built their sacred places must have had specific advantages for those who used them. But what did they use them for?

One tenacious myth that has taken hold in many a mind is that the prehistoric temples and stone circles were used as astronomical observatories. This idea has been going the rounds since the late 19th century, when archaeologists first recognized the way that Stonehenge, on Salisbury Plain in England, was built to coincide with a number of seasonal astronomical events. It was full of 'sightlines' between the stones to significant sunrises, sunsets, phases of the Moon, and movements of the stars.

Many of the conclusions drawn by the early pioneers of astro-archaeology have since been found to be – not to put too fine a point on it – wildly wrong. In spite of this, their ideas were revived in the 1960s. It is in fact illogical and outmoded to believe that a place like Stonehenge could have been used to watch and mark the behaviour of the Sun and Moon and stars.

The illogic of such an idea is easily exposed, for to build these sites in the first place, someone must have known beforehand all the astronomical phenomena to which their stones are so precisely aligned. The builders of the great prehistoric monuments had already made their observations of the sky and taken their measurements on the ground long before they laid a single stone. It is an especially piquant notion that such a massive construction as Stonehenge could ever have had the flexibility that is essential to a real observatory. Such places are not evidence of some kind of primitive science, as the first researchers believed, and as many who mourn for the 1960s still do today.

'No astronomer-priests surveyed the skies there,' Professor Aubrey Burl has written plainly of Stonehenge. 'Superstition, not science, dominated the minds of its builders.'

COSMIC DRAMA

Not only did the ancients see the material world in a different way from us, they seem to have found a link between space and time, and between solid reality and the realm of the spirit. Ancient astronomy was a religious quest, and Stonehenge is one of the most dramatic and visible pieces of evidence of that. Its role was not that of being a record or marker of a scientific view of the Universe and the Earth within it. It was built as a stone stage set for a cosmic drama. But by the time it reached its most complex form in stone, it was not even the greatest of such constructions in the ancient world.

Stonehenge seems to be a symbol of enormous stability, and that it is a monument to an apprehension of cosmic reality that has long since been lost only makes the splendour of the place, emptied now of its original meaning, all the more moving. But the toppled stones and magnificent relics of grandeur that we see today are in reality the last and, amazingly, the least complicated of a series of temples that were built on this single site over a period of some 16 centuries.

A TEMPLE OF DEATH

The very first Stonehenge was made not of stone, but of earth. Around 3200 BC the skin-clad peasants of the farming tribes of Salisbury Plain dug out a wide circular earthwork known as a henge. It had an inner bank broken by what seemed to be two entrances. One was 35 ft wide on the north-east arc of the henge. The second was narrower, and was set precisely south of the centre of the henge. The builders probably found this point by halving the distance between the points on the horizon where the midwinter Sun rose and set.

In 1723 the antiquarian William Stukeley (who also

Stonehenge is perhaps the most impressive of all megalithic monuments – yet its architectural splendour hides the slow spiritual decay of those who built it.

discovered the other great prehistoric site in southern England, Avebury) noticed that the south-west to north-east axis of this original construction, and thus the north-eastern 'entrance', was almost in line with the midsummer sunrise. Later researchers realized that Stukeley had made an error. The builders had been interested in another heavenly body: not the Sun, but the Moon.

Outside the north-east gap in the earthwork each year, they had set up a post in line with the most northerly rising-point of the Moon. Unlike the rising-point of the midsummer Sun, this moves gradually across the horizon between two extremes, over a period of 18.61 years. The ancient builders had recorded this slow motion over six cycles and more than a century of observations, until they were certain of the most northerly point where the Moon rose. They aligned one side of the north-east 'entrance' with this point.

The first Stonehenge was a temple to the Moon. It was also a temple of death.

ROTTING CORPSES

For more than a millennium the ancestors of the first builders of Stonehenge had buried their dead in long barrows that pointed to the Moon somewhere between its midwinter rising-point in the north and its midsummer rising in the south. For these people, death and the Moon were inextricably bound up together.

The north-east 'entrance' was in fact a window, one side aligned to the midpoint of the Moon's arc, the other to its northernmost rising. Marking these lines of sight were pairs of tall stones at the edges of the causeway. On its eastern side the middle of the lunar cycle was marked by the now-fallen Slaughter Stone. The famous Heel Stone, beyond it, was never a pointer for the midsummer sunrise. It was always a lunar marker.

At the centre of the first Stonehenge was a 100 ft wide roofed building where corpses were laid until their flesh had rotted, and then the bones would be buried in the long barrows on the plain outside. This rite was long practised in Neolithic Britain and was always associated with the Moon.

The power of this strange holy mortuary was enhanced by more dead, deliberately acquired. In ditches at the ends of both entrances through the earthwork lie the bones of adults and children, sacrificed to the cold-faced, sky-sailing, shape-shifting silvery goddess of death that these people worshipped.

A TEMPLE OF THE SUN

Around 2200 BC, a new people arrived in the region and converted Stonehenge into a temple of the Sun. Whether they were a branch of what archaeologists call Beaker Folk or not, their characteristic remains are bright-red, geometrically patterned beaker pots. Teams of men bagged Welsh bluestones into the already ancient earthen enclosure and set them up in two concentric circles. Some of the slabs were shaped as lintels, imitating the earlier timber building.

The stones themselves had come from the Preseli mountains in south-west Wales. Legend said they were brought the 200 miles from those bleak, rainswept hills by none other than Merlin, the mysterious guardian mage of Camelot and King Arthur. Later, theories as elaborate as any concocted to account for the building of the pyramids in Egypt sprang fully formed from the brains of unwary academics to explain the logistics of moving the giant blocks to Salisbury Plain in an age that lacked the wheel. The favourite theory had copper prospectors hauling the things on logs and floating them down rivers.

The real history of Stonehenge is full of surprises. The intrepid-stone-age-trucker theory is even less likely to be true than the rather more pleasing image of Merlin wafting the stones across the Severn with his wand. Archaeologists have found a Welsh bluestone in a barrow that was abandoned ten centuries before Stonehenge was built, yet only seven miles from the site. The prosaic truth is that the bluestones were literally lying about the local landscape, waiting to be used by anyone who was minded to do so. They were dumped there by glacial action, perhaps as long as 8,000 years before Stonehenge was even thought of.

The people who brought the stones changed the axis of the henge. They widened the right-hand side of the north-east 'entrance', so that the middle of the break in the earthwork was now in line with the midsummer sunrise. On either side of the Heel Stone, they dug an avenue that led downhill towards the River Avon.

For these people, beakers and Sun worship went together. Tissue-thin discs of gold have been found with the pots in their distinctive round barrows and are decorated with circles and crosses, and they seem to be symbols of the Sun.

The newcomers placed four stones at the corners of a large rectangle around the unfinished stone circles. Now called the Four Stations, these created three sightlines. The short side of the rectangle they made indicated the midsummer sunrise, while the long side pointed to the northern moonset. Down the line of one diagonal one saw – can still see – the point on the horizon where the Sun sets on May Day, later to be celebrated by the Celts as another Sun festival, Beltane, which means 'the shining one'.

Death was still the essential reason for the existence of the rearranged temple. The burials round about, in the new round barrows, continued apace, dug with sweat and toil from the chalky downland. And on the new axis of the henge, not far from the centre of the stone circles, the newcomers dug the grave of a man, and laid his bone in it with the head to the north-west, looking towards the midsummer Sun. His life gave life and strength – it consecrated – the magical place on the borderline between here and there, the present and the future.

THE SUNSET OF STONEHENGE

At the height of the Early Bronze Age, around 2000 BC, Stonehenge was remade yet again – into the form whose battered and crumbling remains we can see today. By then, great cemeteries of round barrows were crowded into the landscape around the temple. In them lay the bodies of chieftains and their women, clothed in finely woven wool, with their weapons, and household items made of bronze, copper, jet, amber, faience and gold. In a few centuries Stonehenge had changed from being a simple peasant mortuary chapel to a grand cathedral, the exclusive last resting-place of the rich, the powerful, the hard and the mighty.

The Moon, not the Sun, was the most important heavenly body to the builders of the first Stonehenge.

One might speculate easily on how the new Stonehenge was pressured into being. Possibly the warrior chieftains had grumbled about the poor place the temple was, until their demands forced a monument befitting their status from a servile priesthood and a crushed people. Possibly the priests themselves had become the real powers behind these tiny thrones, and flaunted their power in this last grand architectural gesture. In any case, Stonehenge was rebuilt, but it was no longer a place for the common people. It became weighty and overwhelming, with room only for the priests, their acolytes, and the privileged.

The bluestones were torn out at the roots. From the Marlborough Downs, 20 miles away, gangs of the faithful or coerced somehow found the energy to drag massive sandstone blocks to the site, where they were shaped and erected in the circle that everyone now knows as Stonehenge. Thirty uprights supported 30 lintels. These stones, bizarrely, were finished by using carpentry techniques – as if no one knew how to dress stone, and as if the builders could not tear themselves away from the memory that this site had once sported a timber building. Inside this forbiddingly atavistic ring of stones, in a monstrous horseshoe pattern, were set five trilithons, five separate, towering archways, each of two pillars topped by a lintel.

The axis of the henge was reversed yet again. The horseshoe of trilithons was open to the north-east but rose in height towards the tallest of them, to the south-west, where the Sun would be seen setting at midwinter – but only by the few for whom there was room in this spectacular but now cramped and darkened place. Astronomically, it was, quite literally, but a gigantic shadow of its former self. The only cosmic matter of interest to its priests was the single alignment to the midwinter sunset.

Whole epic novels might be written about how the mighty slowly but surely toppled after that. The process took 1,000 years, and no doubt the last of them were the most tragic, dramatic, bloody and meaningless. The system decayed; the great stones became empty at the heart. By 1000 BC Stonehenge had been deserted. The place was left to the shrieking crows, the wind, and the teeth of the rain – and to the curiosity of those who came nearly 30 centuries later, and wondered what the place had ever been for.

ANCIENT LIGHTS

The builders of the ancient sites did not create them all solely as places from which to peer out and watch the Sun and Moon performing in predictable order. The events and effects they designed them for may have been predictable, but they could be far more spectacular than a mere moonrise or a sunset. One of the ways the ancients celebrated their festival days was to create dramatic lighting effects within the very monuments themselves.

These ancient lightshows, as veteran Earth mysteries researcher Paul Devereux has dubbed them, needed a dark stone interior for their full effect to be seen and felt, and, without exception, they were designed to form part of some kind of religious ritual. A good example of this mixture of exploiting astronomical observation and religious significance can still be seen at Burro Flats in the Simi Hills, near Los Angeles, California. Here, a panel of Chumash Indian rock paintings marks the site of a long-dead medicine man's shrine. The paintings are of centipede-like creatures, winged human forms, clawed animals, and handprints. These are traditional and ancient signs of sanctity in American Indian lore.

For most of the year, rock overhangs shelter the paintings at Burro Flats but, on midwinter's day, the rising Sun sends a shaft of light through a natural gap in the rocks that surround the shrine, pointing a pencil of light across the paintings. Thus the inner world of the Earth and of human art, spirit, the emotions and the mind – and the outer world of the sky and its heavenly bodies were linked.

Nowhere is this link between the inner and the outer universe made more clearly or more spectacularly than at the complex of monuments in the Boyne Valley, Ireland. The best known of these is the vast Newgrange mound, which is a huge construction penetrated by secret passages and chambers whose ultimate purpose can only be guessed at. Inside the mound, a passage 60 ft long leads to a high stone chamber at

87

the heart of the mound. Here, the rising midwinter Sun sends its light through a roof-box built above the entrance to the passage. Only on midwinter's day can the beam of sunlight reach to the back of this central chamber.

On the Loughcrew Hills of Ireland, US artist Mark Brennan and his research colleagues found that at the equinox – the two days in the year when night and day are of equal duration – the rising Sun shines into a cairn there, and that it frames a rock carving at the back of the inner chamber. The carving was a neolithic symbol for the Sun. The eight rays emanating from its centre represented the eight ancient divisions of the year.

The temple builders of Neolithic Europe used this kind of effect in many sacred mounds. The entrance passage of Maes Howe, Orkney, for instance, is aligned with the midwinter sunset. The passage forms part of an intricate web of alignments that cover the whole island.

Inside the 5,000-year-old stone chamber of Gavrinis in northern France, a block of quartz stands exactly halfway along the length of the entrance passage. It can hardly be an accident that it was placed at a point where the beams from the sunrise, pouring down the passage at midwinter, would intersect those from the Moon at a key point in the 19-year lunar cycle. Archaeologist Aubrey Burl suggests that the builders of Gavrinis used quartz in this place because it would glow dramatically white when the Sun and moonbeams played on it.

THE HEART OF THE EARTH

Similar effects were put to work at the temple of Karnak in Egypt. Much of the surviving temple complex dates from the New Kingdom (1567–1085 BC), but the place was regarded as sacred for centuries before that. Through all its long history, the major astronomical axis of the site remained the same. In the

1890s, the astronomer Sir Norman Lockyer calculated that this axis pointed towards the midsummer sunset. He pictured the dying rays of the Sun reaching in to illuminate the image of the god kept in the darkened sanctuary that lay on the axis deep within the temple.

In the southern hemisphere is the Torreon, in the Inca citadel of Machu Picchu, Peru. The north-eastern window of the inner sanctum of the temple was cut to receive the beams of the midwinter sunrise (which occurs on 21 June in the southern hemisphere). Beneath this inner window is an altar-like rock that has been carved so that a sharp cleft, at right angles to the window, divides it in half. When the Sun rises at midwinter, its light floods in through the window, falling parallel to the cleft. It is possible that originally a frame hung from the carved knobs that protrude from the otherwise featureless wall in the Torreon, supporting a plumb line that would have thrown its shadow along the cut edge on the altar stone at the same time as the slice of sunlight lit it up.

On a ledge near the top of the 430 ft high Fajada Butte in Chaco Canyon, New Mexico, three fallen slabs of rock allow sharp shafts of sunlight through onto the rock wall behind them. A thousand years ago the Anasazi Indians (who lived here and to whom the place was sacred) carved two spirals into the rock face so that these 'Sun daggers' would cast their shadows on them in distinctive patterns at the equinoxes and at midsummer and midwinter.

Further west along Chaco Canyon is the ruin of the Anasazi's great kiva, Casa Rinconada. This 12 ft deep, 63 ft wide circular ceremonial structure was built so that it lay north–south, east–west, and like Stonehenge has an opening in its wall to the north-east. The rising midsummer Sun casts a beam of light through this aperture onto the opposite wall of the kiva, illuminating one of six irregularly spaced wall niches.

The stepped pyramid at Chichen Itza, Mexico, comes alive at the equinoxes as light and shadow create a representation of Kukulcan, the feathered serpent to which it is dedicated.

The ancient builders thus symbolized how the outer universe of Sun and Moon always penetrates to the heart of the Earth. But this truth, which is reminiscent of the black and white dots in the ancient Chinese yin/yang symbol, was a fact of life to these people, whose lives reflected the constant interaction of both. Earth and sky were but aspects of the same thing to them.

THE HITCHING POST OF THE SUN

As the Sun gives light, so it also casts shadows. This fact was not lost on the ancients in their ceremonies and in the way they built their sacred places.

In Mexico, the Indians used shadow in a particularly flamboyant fashion, and with perfect symbolism. The so-called Castillo at Chichen Itza on the Yucatan peninsula is a Toltec-Mayan stepped pyramid originally dedicated to Kukulcan, the feathered serpent god. A spectacular light-and-shadow picture forms on the Castillo at the spring and summer equinoxes. In the last hour before sunset, the stepped, north-west corner of the pyramid throws a serrated shadow onto the west-facing balustrade of its northern staircase. This produces a pattern of sunlight and shadow that looks strikingly like the body markings of the rattlesnake common to the region. At the bottom of the balustrade are serpents' heads, carved in stone. To these the shadow attaches itself, completing the image of the sacred snake, writhing down the holy pyramid.

In the last refuge of the Incas, the mountain-peak citadel at Machu Picchu, Peru, the small but highly significant Intihuatana is carved from a granite outcrop that sits on a naturally pyramid-shaped spur. The Intihuatana is an upright pillar, no more than a foot high, projecting from a complex, asymmetrical platform made up of a variety of odd surfaces and projections.

The name Intihuatana means 'hitching post of the Sun', which is a sure indication that this strangely fashioned (or adapted) feature must have played a vital part in the major Inca festival of Inti Raymi. This took place every winter solstice – the shortest day of the year – to 'tie the Sun'. The ritual prevented the Sun from moving any further north in its daily round and stopped it being lost for ever.

SHADOWS OF THE SUN

At Ireland's Newgrange, the American artist Martin Brennan noted something else besides the entry of the midwinter sunbeam into the great mound. He found that the entrance stone and another 'kerbstone 52' were part of the solar alignment of the site, and that some of the stones in the huge stone circle surrounding the mound also play a part in creating astonishing light-and- shadow effects on that crucial day of the year. And it was crucial: the prehistoric people of the Old World, like the Incas in Peru half a world away, also feared that the Sun might disappear for ever at midwinter.

At midwinter sunrise, as the roof-box at the entrance directs the Sun's rays deep into the mound, the shadow of one of the circle's stones points like a finger to the entrance stone and its vertical marking. At the same time, the shadow from a nearby stone strikes another carved kerbstone. With the complex interplay of shadow and light at the site, it is, as one commentator has said, 'almost as if the builders of Newgrange have left software running in their hardware'.

At nearby Knowth, another mound built like Newgrange with an inner passage and central chamber (and at about the same time, around 3700 BC), Brennan discovered that when the Sun sets at the equinoxes and sends its light down the entrance passage, a standing stone outside likewise throws its shadow onto the vertically grooved entrance stone.

At Castlerigg stone circle in Cumbria, England, photographer John Glover saw an extraordinary phenomenon during the midsummer sunset in 1976. Just as the Sun was sinking to the ridge on the horizon, Glover glanced behind him, and was amazed to see that the tallest stone of the circle was throwing a huge shadow right across the valley.

When the path of the shadow was surveyed later, the researchers found that the slope of the ground beyond the site was such that the shadow fell parallel to it and so extended far beyond the immediate ground. A conifer plantation stands in the way today, but originally it would have stretched for more than two miles across the moor.

THE LIGHT IN THE DARKNESS

Can we deduce anything from these alignments and angles, the subtle interplay of light and shade, or even from the final dark centuries of Stonehenge, with its fixation on midwinter and death, about the meaning of these astonishing constructions?

The answer is, tentatively at least, yes. As was remarked earlier, the symbolism of these ancient places indicates that for those who fashioned them with such care and attention, Earth and sky were not separate, but parts of a whole. There is more to be quarried here, however. Even the monumental morbidity of Stonehenge speaks of a fixation with wholeness – and by implication with balance, as if the ancients had anticipated and written in stone and ritual the words of Cranmer's prayerbook: 'In the midst of life we are in death...'

In the same way, the penetrating light of the Sun at sites all over the world is balanced by shadows; the dark created by light, the light known only in the darkness of a hidden chamber. Earth and cosmos were tied together by threads of light and a network of shadows in a kind of symbiosis. The one could not exist without the other, the ancients saw, and dramatized their intuition in their sacred architecture.

To them, Earth, Sun and Moon coexisted in a cosmic marriage. Part of the drama played out by the stones is conjugal: the long hard light of the Sun penetrating the secret passage of the Earth; the phallic shadow stretching itself and growing across the surface of the Earth's vast body. This was not a crass cartoon, a huge slide-show of sex and fertility, but an enactment of ultimate cosmic union.

And wherever this celebration of balance, of wholeness, of cosmic passion took place, the people could see that they were at the centre of the Universe, for here all things met as one. The ancient places were at the core of all existence.

THE MYSTIC LANDSCAPE

For the ancients the Earth was a woman – a mother to be worshipped and cherished, and a lover to be erotically embraced. The secret places of her body were the most sacred sites of the pagan religions, but their true purpose remains mysterious…

A sense of centrality inspired the builders of the world's ancient monuments: they treated their creations as if they truly were at the centre of things, and placed them where the whole surrounding landscape reinforced and reflected that feeling. If need be they would mould whole landscapes to underline the importance of a particular site.

The image of the world's centre took a number of forms in the ancient world. One was the omphalos, the navel of the world. Another was the 'world egg'. Another was the 'world tree'. Derived from the Tree of Life were any number of more portable icons and symbols: particular, living, sacred trees, or so-called totem poles, or even a simple rod stuck in the Earth. Wherever these were, there – for the purpose at hand - was the centre of the world.

Marking that central point of the world was the first great magical act in creating sacred geography. Its spiritual importance is nowhere better illustrated than in the creation myth of the Zuni American Indians of New Mexico, who are probably descended from the Anasazi who built Chaco Canyon.

According to their myth, the first Zuni wandered for a long time, looking for a place of peace and stability, where they would settle. Frustrated in their search, they finally summoned *K'yan asdebi*, the water-skate, because his long legs could point in all the directions. A centre of a kind himself, he could surely identify the centre of the world.

This he did. He rose into the sky and stretched out his legs in the six great directions: the four cardinal points of the compass, and above and below. Gradually he came back to Earth, saying, 'Where my heart and navel rest, beneath them mark the spot and there build a town of the midmost, for there shall be the midmost place of the Earth-mother, even the navel...'

A VIEW OF THE GODS

The idea of the sacred centre is really an extension of the individual's perception that he or she already exists at the centre of his or her own world. Each of us looks out upon the world with an intuitive idea of six basic directions: front, back and sides, with the Earth beneath our feet, and the heavens above us. Wherever we are, we are always at the centre of our world.

At its deepest level, the meaning of a sacred site made itself felt through the action of the landscape on the mind, and the reaction of the mind to the landscape. Ultimate reality could not be apprehended without this exchange between mind and landscape. The place represented a whole that fused together three things: time – made visible as a result of the astronomical alignments of the place, and its play of light and shadow; space, in the form of the landscape that reflected the work of the gods; and man-made imagery, the sign of human consciousness and awareness.

The sacred centre was sacred exactly because it was the place from which the movements of the Sun and Moon were observed and measured against the skyline, and because it was the place from which the actions of the gods – sometimes, even their very shapes – could be witnessed. It was the centre because all things were joined there.

THE ORACLE OF DELPHI

The best-known omphalos in the Old World is the temple complex, sanctuary and ancient home of the oracle at Delphi, Greece. According to Greek myth, Delphi was founded after the chief of the gods, Zeus, sent out two eagles from the far ends of the Earth; where their flights crossed would be the centre of the world. The eagles met over Mount Parnassos, on whose southern slopes Delphi was built.

Reflecting this legend, some classic depictions of omphalos stones (which existed at numerous sacred sites in ancient Greece) show two birds perched on them, facing in opposite directions. Two such stones survive at Delphi today. One is in the complex of temple ruins and is a cone of grey stone shot through with quartz veins. The other is now in Delphi's museum. It is egg-shaped, about 3 ft high, and covered by a delicate interlaced pattern carved in bas-relief.

THE STOREHOUSE OF THE DEAD

The Andean Indians have a very different concept of the stars in the sky from the Western notion of a series of constellations like a picture-book of mythical beings. To the Quechua Indian community of Misminay, who live near the Vilcanota river, about 30 miles north-west of Cuzco, Peru, the Milky Way is the key feature of the night sky.

They call the Milky Way Mayu, 'River'. They see it as the heavenly version of their River Vilcanota, which flows from south-east to north-west, and in Quechua myth is said to dump its waters off the edge of the Earth into the encircling void of the heavens. These waters are collected in the north-west by the Milky Way which carries them through the sky before letting them fall to Earth and rise again in the east. As the waters are carried overhead, some of the moisture drops to Earth again as rain. The terrestrial and celestial rivers fertilize land and sky.

From Misminay (as from any fixed point on the Earth), the Milky Way appears to swing across the sky, so that every 12 hours its southern and northern ends respectively appear to rise from the south-east and north-east. In a 24-hour period, this apparent movement draws two lines across the sky that

Sioux Indians in an ecstatic dance, with their medicine man or shaman in buffalo hide. The centre of the cosmos for the Sioux is Mount Harney, and the shaman's staff is also a symbol of the 'world axis' around which Heaven and Earth revolve.

intersect directly overhead. The Quechua call this zenith point Cruz Calvario, the 'cross of Calvary', borrowing the term from Christian missionaries, whose work among them was not entirely successful.

This division of space by the Milky Way is reflected on the ground in the layout of the Misminay settlement itself. Two footpaths and irrigation canals running side by side form an X-shaped cross on the ground. Their intersection is called Crucero, 'the cross'. This corresponds to the 'crossing point' of the Milky Way in the sky overhead – Calvario. Crucero is the place in Misminay from where the horizons of the 'four quarters' of the world are marked by the local people. Each direction is meaningful in Quechua mythology, and the meaning of each is reflected in house groupings in the village and in the significance the people give to certain sacred peaks beyond. The north-west–north-east quarter, for example, is associated with the ancestors, and the holy mountain on the horizon in that direction is called Apu Wanumarka, the 'Storehouse of the Dead'. Here again we have a linking of Earth and sky, life and death, past and future, the interpenetration of space and time in which each part gains its meaning and nourishes the spirit only because it is part of the whole image of the Universe that the people entertain.

THE GOLDEN NAVEL OF THE EARTH

Most ancient peoples possessed some concept of the sacred centre, and it could take many forms. It could be stone, as at Delphi or Delos in Greece, a holy city like the Incas' Cuzco (the name means 'navel' in the Quechua tongue), or a rock, as it is for the Semangs of the Malay Peninsula, where Batu-Ribn emerges at the centre of the world. It is a rock, too, at Jerusalem, that great centre sacred to Judaism, Christianity and Islam alike, and it is a rock too in Mecca.

The world centre could also be a peak, a 'world mountain'. To the Sioux Indians of the American Great Plains, the centre of the world was on Mount Harney. Israel may boast three world centres including Jerusalem – Mount Tabor, whose name may mean 'navel', according to the historian Mircea Eliade, and Mount Gerizim, which, Eliade maintains, was 'undoubtedly invested with the prestige of the centre, for it is called "navel of the earth". Buddhists too have their world centre in Mount Kailash in Tibet, the legendary 'Mount Meru', centre of the cosmos to believers. People still make pilgrimages to the remote mountain, to make a ritual tour around it. Some even make the circuit on their knees. In Japan, the volcanic cone of Mount Fujiyama is sacred; the Shinto religion centres on living earth mysteries.

The notion of the holy peak is deeply embedded in the human psyche. Croagh Padric in the west of Ireland, sacred to the great Christian saint of the island, is likewise a centre of pilgrimages and rituals, which are possibly not Christian at all in origin but an adaptation of a far older tradition.

Besides appearing in stones, rocks and mountains, the centre of the world might be represented by a pole, or even a pit dug in the ground. The 'world tree', in particular, was a universal form of the sacred centre. The world tree connected the heavens and the underworld, but was also the axis from which the middle world, the Earth, orientated itself. It was the

Mount Fujiyama, Japan's sacred mountain whose volcanic nature makes it a prime symbol of the raw power hidden within the Earth.

'still point of the turning world', but also a kind of conducting rod between the upper and lower parts of the whole cosmos.

The Yakut tribes of Siberia believe that at the 'golden navel of the Earth' stands a tree with eight branches. In Norse and Old German mythology, the world tree was named Yggdrasil, and trees that symbolize the sacred centre live on in traditions as diverse and distant from one another as those of the Australian aborigines and American Indians.

Like the sacred mountain, the roots of the world tree reach into the human mind, and the sap still rises in this ancient image. It is found in (relatively) modern opera, in Wagner's reworking of the German myths in *The Ring*, and even in English literature. In *Women In Love*, written in the 1920s, D.H. Lawrence was still conjuring with the tree of life as a symbol of growth, wholeness and spiritual stability, at whose roots gnaw the corruptions of modern 'civilization'.

A SLEEPING BEAUTY

Gazing out from their cosmic centre across the landscape, the ancients saw a very different world from the one we think we are looking at. Agriculture, where it existed, was neither a cosy calling pursued by a romanticized minority nor a business, but a battle with nature that involved most of the tribe most of the time. Nor were the deserts dead but photogenic places. The whole of the landscape was alive.

Since Earth and the heavens enacted a cosmic marriage, it is not surprising that many ancient peoples around the world saw in the hills and moors, deserts and mountains around them the shape of a vast goddess, the Earth Mother. She did not give life to the land; she was its life, and they saw her in it.

The island of Jura off the west coast of Scotland has a range of mountains called the Paps: the central peaks are symmetrical and rounded like breasts. At Ballochroy, on the Kintyre peninsula on the mainland, the central stone of three menhirs has a smoothed side that faces the most northerly of the Paps, Beinn Corra, 19 miles distant across the sound. Behind this peak the Sun sets at midsummer.

On Lewis, the most north-westerly of the major Hebrides islands, the Pairc Hills are known locally as the 'Sleeping Beauty': they resemble the profile of a woman lying on her back. From the cluster of stone circles and settings known as the Stones of Callanish, it seems that when the Moon rises at its most southerly point during its 19-year cycle, it comes forth from the Pairc Hills. At this one time in the cycle it is as if the Sleeping Beauty gives birth to the Moon.

Two symmetrical, rounded hills near Killarney, Ireland, are known as the Paps of Anu. In the Irish myths, Anu is the mother of the last generation of gods to rule the Earth, the legendary Tuatha de Danaan. According to Celtic scholar Dr Anne Ross, these hills are still regarded with awe today. They 'personify the powers of the goddess embedded in the land', and Anu 'is still regarded as the local fairy queen'.

From the Greek island of Poros, off the north-east coast of the Peloponnisos, the mountains on the mainland are seen by local people as outlining the form of a woman lying on her back. 'The resemblance is indeed persuasive,' says the American historian Vincent Scully almost primly in *The Earth, the Temple and the Gods*, although he notes with some relish the shapes of 'the head low on the north, a long neck, high breasts, arched stomach, long legs with the knees drawn up'.

UPLIFTED BREASTS

In *Symbolic Landscapes*, Earth mysteries scholar Paul Devereux draws attention to the vast number of Bronze Age Cretan figurines that exist of a goddess with her arms raised in a characteristic and apparently curious gesture. The best-known example is the faience Snake Goddess found at Knossos, the heart of the ancient Minoan empire on Crete. Both the figure's upraised arms and its breasts, emphasized by an open bodice, create a cleft shape that is a direct echo of the sacred landscape of the island. The courtyard of the palace at Knossos opens to the distant, cleft-peaked Mount Yiouktas. The palace's propylaia or entrance is precisely aligned with the mountain.

The Minoan bull ritual, in which young men and women seized the horns of a charging bull and were propelled over its back, also echoed the horned peak of Mount Yiouktas. We know about the ritual because it is detailed in frescos found at Knossos, and it was performed under the eye of the horned mountain.

'The landscape and temples together form [an] architectural whole,' Vincent Scully wrote of the ancient Greeks' perception of their surroundings. He believed that the Greeks had 'developed an eye' for 'specific combinations of landscape features as expressive of particular holiness'.

This perception of the interchangeability of land and spirit was not confined to Knossos by any means. Other Cretan palaces were built in a deliberate relationship with horned mountains. Among them are Mama, which points toward Mount Gikte, and Phaistos, which is aligned to Mount Ida. At Gournia, the palace faces two hills that Scully described as 'so close and rounded that a more proper analogy would seem to be more directly to the female body itself and they do closely resemble the uplifted breasts' of the goddess. He remarked too that the enclosed landscape around Gournia gave the 'inescapable impression' that the palace was being embraced in the arms of the Earth Mother.

Similarly, the characteristic gesture in representations of the goddess is found throughout the Mediterranean. The small terracotta goddess figurines of Mycenae on the Greek mainland have the same raised arms. Tombs in the Castelluccio cemetery in Sicily were carved to show a powerful figure with upraised arms, breasts and head. Pieces of pottery of the same period from Sicily, the Lipari Islands and southern Italy all have horn-like handles to create an image of a goddess with raised arms.

The motif is thousands of years old. Female figurines and pottery decorations from pre-dynastic Egypt, for instance, feature this sacred gesture of upraised arms. The psychologist Erich Neumann has suggested that this universally repeated gesture of the Earth Mother indicates prayer, invocation or a magical conjuring of the deity. What he might have added is the reflection that it also reinforces the impression that the ancients saw their world as a cosmic union in which spiritual energy is constantly cycling through the whole of creation.

For it can hardly be insignificant that the goddess is always portrayed as herself in an attitude of worship. The Earth Mother was not separate from the rest of the Universe complacently receiving its supplications but herself takes part in a mutual – and mutually invigorating – reverence. Time and space, people, gods, spiritual energy, Earth, Sun, Moon and landscape were all aspects of one another. The world was whole, and holy.

HOLY LINES

Of all the conundrums posed by the anciet world's mystical landscapes, the most baffling is the fact that most are built on, or in, straight lines of one kind or another. This puzzling feature takes many different forms around the world. Every one of them brings us back to one of the most familiar, yet most fundamental, of the 'Earth mysteries': the riddle of 'ley lines'. The usual story is that leys were discovered by Alfred Watkins

The Old Sarum ley in Wiltshire. The photograph shows the ruin of Old Sarum with Salisbury Cathedral in the distance.

one sunny June afternoon in 1921. As the 66-year-old businessman was sitting in his car, gazing out over his native Herefordshire from Blackwardine, he glanced down at the map in front of him. It was then, in a sudden epiphany, that he realized that the prehistoric mounds, earthworks and standing stones of the country before him were arrayed in arrow-straight lines across the landscape.

Watkins was not, in fact, the first to notice this. Numerous researchers had recorded their findings prior to Watkins's 'discovery' of 1921. As early as 1846, for instance, the antiquarian Edward Duke had proposed that Stonehenge and Avebury, some 20 miles apart, were part of an invisible straight line across the countryside that passed through another stone circle and two prehistoric earthworks. Other scholars throughout the 19th century noticed similar alignments, and in

The 'Cliff Palace', the largest of the Anasazi settlements perched high within the escarpment at Mesa Verde in southern Colorado.

1904, Hilaire Belloc published *The Old Road*, in which he described medieval pilgrimage routes linking old churches in England and, drawing on his observations while travelling in the USA, the straight tracks of American Indians.

Watkins, however, provided a comprehensive account for the ancient lines on the land. He believed they were the remaining signs of prehistoric traders' trackways, and they were straight because they had been laid out by line-of-sight. Watkins kept finding distinctive boulders on the lines he explored. He was convinced these were part of the original, prehistoric survey, and consequently called them 'markstones'. He also found old churches and crosses on the alignments which, he argued, were pagan – i.e. prehistoric – sacred places that had been commandeered by Christianity.

Watkins called his alignments 'leys' because he noted the word recurring in placenames on the lines. It comes from the Welsh word llan, which originally meant 'sacred enclosure'. The possible significance of this passed Watkins by, possessed as he was, like any good Victorian merchant, with the idea that the leys must have been trade routes. But the point was not lost on his contemporaries, the German researchers Josef Heinsch, who noted lines linking hills and old churches, and Wilhelm Teudt, who called the German alignments he discovered *heilige Linien*, 'holy lines'.

MYSTERIOUS ROADS TO NOWHERE

As Hilaire Belloc had realized, mysterious straight lines running through the landscape between ancient sites, and utterly regardless of their practicability as paths as they shot up sheer inclines and blithely disappeared over precipices, were not an exclusively European phenomenon. And as research and surveying and archaeological digs continued, it became apparent that nowhere are there such enigmatic lines in the landscape as in the Americas.

The American Indians of antiquity made what are literally old straight tracks – they too ignored practicality for the sake of a ruler-like precision – and equally straight lines of sacred sites, shrines, holy rocks and wells. The remains of this curious practice can be seen all over the Americas, and it obsessed many diverse and distant American Indian cultures. One of the most intriguing of all these prehistoric straightline systems is in the American South-west: the 'Chaco roads'.

These are centred on Chaco Canyon, in the high mesa country of north-west New Mexico. They were made by the Anasazi, whose name is actually a Navajo Indian term meaning 'the enemies of our ancestors'. The Anasazi thrived in the Four Quarters area of New Mexico from about AD 800 to about 1300; some of them, in these latter years, clashed with the Navajo as they migrated into the region from AD 1000. The Anasazi developed a distinctive style of flat-roofed buildings made of mud, rock and wood, called pueblos.

Chaco Canyon was the prime Anasazi ceremonial centre. Here, the culture reached its height. Over the years, the pueblos grew into multi-storeyed terraced complexes now known as 'Great Houses', with walls, courtyards, and 'Great Kivas' – very large ceremonial chambers. There are nine Great Houses within Chaco Canyon itself, all built between AD 900 and 1115. The largest was Pueblo Bonito, covering some three acres.

CARVED THROUGH LIVING ROCK

The Anasazis' mysterious roads radiate in straight lines for many miles around Chaco Canyon. They are fully engineered, a fairly constant 30 ft wide, with spur roads about half as wide. At their borders are earthen ridges, lines of stones or drystone walls. Their surfaces were laid with compacted earth – or cut straight into the bedrock. The true extent of the Chaco roads became apparent only in the 1970s, when aerial photography revealed how vast the network was. With ground surveys and digs, archaeologists have now mapped some 400 miles of these enigmatic highways.

Like similar sacred 'routes' elsewhere, the Anasazi roads are no respecters of difficult terrain if it stands in their way. When they reached the canyon walls, the Anasazi engineers carved staircases up to 25 ft wide from the living rock, straight down the canyon sides.

The Chaco roads throw up a host of questions. Why did a people with neither horses nor the wheel need these elaborate highways? Are they roads as such at all? Recent computer-enhanced infra-red aerial pictures taken by NASA only deepen the mystery. These have revealed the existence of rows of sections running parallel to the roads. What were they for?

There is a consensus among archaeologists and scholars that the roads were ceremonial or sacred ways that linked the Great Houses, which seem to have been ritual centres. Fragments of pottery have been found In limited areas along some of the roads, notably near Great Houses. Breaking pottery vessels has been an act of consecration in numerous societies in widely distant places all over the world. It was often associated with the dead. It is possible that the Anasazi considered the roads themselves to be holy. It remains – officially at least – a mystery as to who used them, and why they were so broad and so finely made.

The most enigmatic road is 50 miles long and runs due north from Chaco Canyon to a particular mound of earth – but why? There seems to be no obvious answer to that question, nor to the purpose of these roads. Just like many other strange artefacts, the roads are assumed to have some super-

Chaco Canyon was home to the Anasazi, ancestors of today's Pueblo people.

naturalistic purpose. But that still brings us no closer to finding the answer as to why a society would put hundreds of man hours into building roads to places where nothing happened. It can only be assumed that they were places of spiritual value where the Anasazis were expecting something monumental to take place – or perhaps it did!

The Anasazis also built enormous houses, some with thousands of rooms with massive five-storey walls which covered many acres. Some of the best examples of these ancient dwellings can be seen in Chaco Canyon National Park. What is even more strange is that after spending hundreds of years carving their homes out of the side of a mountain, the Anasazi simply vanished mysteriously into thin air. Modern scientists are still not certain why these people left their cliff dwellings, though the common belief is that they were either starved out or forced to leave due to a severe drought. What they left behind were symbolic pictographs and petroglyphs on rock walls (*right*).

INVISIBLE HIGHWAYS

Virtually every sacred site in the prehistoric world was linked with others, major or minor, by a radiating network of straight lines. Few were as elaborate or as easily detected in their heyday as the Anasazis' strange highways. Most were invisible, like the leys of Europe – which makes them, in a way, all the more mysterious. In rare cases like the Ohio effigy mounds and the vast drawing-board that covered the desert floor at Nazca, Peru, entire sites were devoted to creating miles of straight lines and, still more bewildering, very precise pictures that could be appreciated only from the air.

In cultures that enjoyed such a comprehensive world-view, and that had such a magical sense of the continuous life rolling through the whole of creation – which today we sterilize and alienate by calling it the 'environment' – the lines, visible or invisible, had to have meaning and that it was possible some form of energy flowed through the leys. Where do they fit in the weft and warp of this most tightly woven of all mythologies?

This has been the greatest enigma of all in the study of the ancient sacred places. It was also, as a handful of researchers have now realized, the biggest clue of all to the meaning and use of the prehistoric sites, and it was staring them in the face all the time.

A MAP FOR THE MIND

Fault lines, strange lights, magnetic and gravitational abnormalities – how do all of these fit together in the world's mysterious places?

So far, we have gathered up various enigmatic bits of information about the world's mysterious ancient places. They were most often built on fault lines, and these are places where strange lights and magnetic and gravitational anomalies abound. We've seen that these places can have bizarre psychic effects on people. Research by Professor Michael Persinger of Laurentian University in Ontario has even suggested that individuals become especially receptive to extrasensory perception in the presence of the phenomena that cling to the ancient sites.

We know too that these places were seen by the people who built them as cosmic centres on which the Sun and Moon were deliberately focused. Most probably, the cosmic light shows

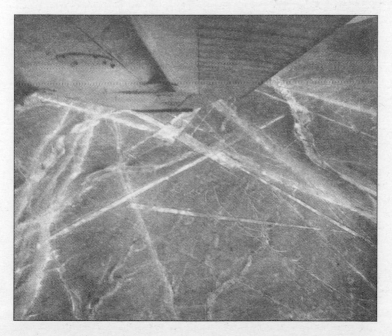

The complexity of the lines and patterns at Nazca becomes clear when they are seen from the air. But why?

were arranged to reinforce the sense of universal centrality of the shrine - its place between the Otherworlds. At the sites, too, the here and now was strangely interfused with the spirit world – whether in the form of the Earth Goddess or through the link between Heaven, Earth and Underworld that was symbolized by the 'world tree' or some other equally potent image. Many sites are associated with the dead. Finally, we have seen that these perplexing places are linked, or infested, by straight lines both visible and invisible.

How, or where, do all these aspects fit together? What is the missing link? A brief tour around one of the most problematic of these baffling monuments may let slip a few more clues.

DESIGNS IN THE DESERT

Probably the most famous of American Indian straight lines are the markings on the desert pampas around Nazca, Peru.

The Nazca lines were drawn by removing the desert surface to reveal the lighter soil beneath. The lines can be anything from a few dozen yards to several miles long, and pass straight over ridges. Intersperzed among the hundreds of straight lines are a variety of line drawings, made in the same way, of animals, sundry geometric forms and irregular and regular abstract shapes.

It is easier to say what the lines and drawings at Nazca are not than to summarise what they might be. That they are not and never did form a landing-strip for 'ancient astronauts' is a statement scarcely worth making: the idea was never worth ten seconds of anyone's time. Nor are the lines aligned to the heavens in any more conventional archaeo-astronomical sense. Work in the 1980s co-ordinated by Anthony F. Aveni of Colgate University, New York State, confirmed the finding by Gerald Hawkins of the Smithsonian Institution in the 1960s that none of the lines had any significant astronomical function.

Aveni and his colleagues did find that there is some pattern to the apparently random layout of the lines on the ground. Nazca's resident researcher Maria Reiche had noted what she called 'star-like centres', from which lines radiated like rays from a sun. Aveni's team identified over 60 of these centres. They are set on natural hills or mounds, and at least one line from each centre connects it with another.

At these 'star-like' centres are deposits of small stones, shells and broken pottery fragments: signs of some kind of offering to the dead, as were found along the 'roads' in Chaco Canyon. In the 1920s, an elder of the Navajo Indians made the cryptic remark to archaeologist Neil Judd that although the Chaco lines looked like roads, they 'were not roads'. The Nazca lines are not tracks, although they look like tracks. They start nowhere and end anywhere.

And the most impenetrable fact of all about Nazca is the line drawings. Why spend energy, which could barely be spared from the hard business of survival, on making pictures that no one could see?

Or could someone see them? And if so – how could they?

PATHWAYS FOR THE SPIRITS

Now let us go back to the straight lines. These are traditionally significant in other contexts. Here is another clue to the hidden meaning of the lines on the Earth – and of the ancient places themselves. There is a very ancient tradition that spirits – good and bad - move in straight lines. There is a huge global lore concerning the usefulness of knots in defending oneself against evil spirits, for instance. But straight lines can be used to encourage the intervention of the most beneficial spirits – most interestingly, in many widespread traditions, by using threads to provide a path for them.

Seen at close quarters, the lines at Nazca seem almost insignificant. Yet enormous energy and devotion went into their design and maintenance. But how did their makers get to see the full effect of their work?

Among some Australian Aboriginal tribes, a healer would treat a sick person by running a spider thread from the head of the 'patient' to a nearby bush. This, said the healer, was where the sufferer's spirit had fled from the ailing body. The filament provided a path for the spirit to return, making the patient whole again and banishing the illness.

Similarly, when dealing with sickness, the shaman (colloquially known as the tribal 'witch doctor' or 'medicine man') of the Buryat peoples of Siberia would place an arrow on the ground beside the patient's head and lay a red thread in a straight line, out through the entrance of the sick person's tent, to a birch pole that he had previously stuck in the ground outside. The pole stood for the world tree, the link between this world and the realms of spirit, while the thread gave the sick person's soul a route along which to return to the body. The principle is almost identical to that of the Australian tradition.

Among the Maoris of New Zealand, the stem of a plant could be taken as a spirit 'line'. The tohunga ('healer') put the stem on a sick person's head and called on the evil spirit that was causing the illness to leave by the 'road' offered by the stem of the plant.

In terms of straight lines, the spirit world and ancient places, the most provocative of all these traditions of healing belongs to the Kalahari !Kung people. When they hold a trance dance, which involves hours of rhythmic movement and continuous chanting in the hypnotic presence of a fire, it's not uncommon for people to leave their bodies – to have what we would call an out-of-the-body experience. The !Kung call this state kia. Once in it, they can climb 'threads' up to 'where God is'. When they are with God, they can become healers. The !Kung say that then they are able to gaze into people's bodies with X-ray vision to see where any disease has taken root, and can then pull it out.

A yarn picture made by the Huichol Indians of central Mexico. In the upper left of the picture are shamans, directing the life force of the Sun's rays as they fall on a cornfield.

Here is a very clear indication that straight lines, contact with the spirit world and a state of trance are all closely related.

THE THREE WORLDS SYSTEM

The key that unlocks the mystery connecting straight lines and the sacred sites lies in the central fact about the ancient places themselves. That is: they were, exactly and literally, central to existence. The sacred centre was not only a place from which to make and take earthly bearings. It linked the 'middle world' of the here and now with the worlds above – Heaven – and below – the Underworld. The realms above and below were kingdoms of the spirit. Anthropologists call this cosmology the 'three worlds system'. It seems to have originated, possibly hundreds of thousands of years ago, with a form of religion known as shamanism.

When and where shamanism began is anyone's guess, but it probably arrived in the Americas with the peoples who migrated across the old land bridge over the Bering Straits somewhere between 15,000 and 25,000 years ago. The shamanic tradition remained strong and healthy among the American Indian tribes until very recent times because the Americas did not suffer the same cultural changes over the centuries as Eurasia did.

What is a shaman? The term itself comes from saman, the word the Tungus peoples of Siberia had for the 'elected member' of the tribe who could journey to the spirit worlds seeking healing for tribal members, finding lost or confused souls or seeking help for those in this world by divining the future or peering into the remote past. The shaman was the intermediary between the tribe and the Otherworld of spirit, and he went to the Otherworld through an out-of-the-body experience. To his conscious self, this experience seemed to be the equivalent of flight above the Earth.

We can infer that this experience of flying was universal from many pieces of evidence. To begin with, shamans all around the world use strikingly similar metaphors to describe their journeys to the Otherworld. They say their spirits rise on smoke, ride along a rainbow, follow a flight of arrows, travel up a sunbeam – and so on. A particularly common image they use is the ladder, stretching from Earth to Heaven – just as Jacob's does in the Bible. He, significantly, also slept on a sacred stone.

ROUTES TO A TRANCE

The shaman used – and still uses – a variety of techniques to achieve the trance state. Among them were prolonged dancing, fasting and chanting. This last, incidentally, was not ordinary chanting. A large choir of Russian Orthodox monks sounds like a tin whistle with the croup in comparison to a shaman in full voice, and the greatest cantor in Brooklyn might as well be a mosquito.

There are few sounds in the world more unearthly than the vocal performance of a Siberian shaman as he prepares to leave the mundane world. Bizarre but distinct whistlings come down from his sinuses and out of his nose and mouth, while he uses an astonishing, fundamental muscular control to produce a grim, low, rhythmic roaring from the diaphragm. On top of these various abnormal noises and mesmeric drones, he manages to produce a conventional human chant, often of eerie beauty, to distract the astounded listener. It comes as something of a surprise to discover that this last, most recognizable, sound is not actually coming out of his ears. The whole effect is both hair-raising and hypnotic, as well as inhuman – as it is surely meant to be, for him as much as for his audience.

Shamans may use other ritual tools at the same time or separately to induce trance. They include exposure to extremes of heat or cold, and a range of more or less horrifying methods of inducing pain and, hence, sensory deprivation. Shamans may also use hallucinogenic plants, foods or smoking mixtures (the 'peace-pipe' had a number of applications, but the ultimate effect was usually very peaceful, not to say positively dreamy).

The hallucinogens that the shamans used are interesting because many of these drugs gave their user a strong impression of flying. One 19th-century explorer into the South American interior described how he felt himself going on 'an aerial journey' as a result of drinking ayahuasaca, a potent Indian tincture made from a hallucinogenic vine. Modern dope slang reflects something of the same experience: among other things, one gets 'high', goes on a 'trip' and gets 'spaced out'.

The mental imagery induced by drug use and trance became central to many tribes' art. Among the rock paintings in a Chumash Indian shrine at Burro Flats, near Los Angeles, California, there is a series of geometric forms – dots, lines, crosses, circles and concentric rings. Similar patterns are found in rock art all over the world, and can be seen carved into the rock at many megalithic sites in Britain.

The source of these patterns is the human brain. The Tukano Indians of Colombia in South America (who use trance-inducing drugs in religious ceremonies) employ similar imagery as a basis for the decorative work on their pottery and clothing, and freely admit that these are based on the colourful but

The biblical image of Jacob's ladder as a connection between the spiritual realm and earthly life is echoed in shamanic traditions throughout the world.

121

geometric forms they see under the influence of the drugs. The San (Bushmen) of the Kalahari, too, make no secret of the fact that the patterns and motifs in their own rock paintings are based on what their shamans see when in trance. These patterns were probably the original inspiration for another enigmatic pattern found at endless numbers of sacred sites all over the world: the labyrinth or maze.

Most significantly, the shaman moved from normal awareness to the Otherworld to the endless beating of a magic drum, which was covered in signs and symbols to protect him on his 'journey' elsewhere. He called his drum his 'steed' or 'canoe' on or in which he would travel to the spirit realm. One of the more intriguing discoveries made about these drums is that they produce sounds at extremely low frequencies – as few as four cycles per second. These affect the so-called theta brain waves, which are somehow involved in the deeper levels of dreaming, trance and meditation.

In the Siberian tribes, the shell of the shaman's drum was, in theory, made from a branch of the world tree (usually, in fact, a birch). Because of this magical link and through his hypnotic drumming, the shaman is 'magically projected into the vicinity of the Tree', as the anthropologist Mircea Eliade put it. In the tribes of central and northern Asia, the shaman would actually climb a birch tree during his trance, to show his spectators that he was indeed ascending the axis of the world and passing into the realm of spirit.

BIRD-MEN THROUGH THE AGES

Once up the tree, he flew. In some tribes, he waved his arms like a bird's wings when he got to the top. During his trance, the Yakut shaman of north-east Siberia also made dance movements and gestures to imitate the flight of a bird.

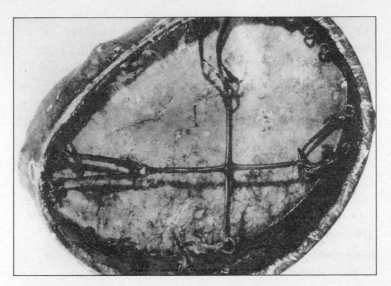

A Siberian shaman's drum. His trance partly induced by its rhythmic reverberations, the shaman believed that the drum became a steed or canoe on which he rode to the Otherworld.

The image of flight was the unmistakable sign of a shaman in the ancient world, and still is in those cultures that have remained prehistoric and pre-industrial in spirit. The most frequent is the form of a bird perched on a stick (standing for the world axis or tree). From this token, the almost unimaginable antiquity of the shaman tradition becomes evident, for among the Cro-Magnon cave paintings of Lascaux, France, there is one of a bird-stick next to a man in a bird mask, who is apparently in trance. The painting may be a quarter of a million years old.

The Mississippian people, who flourished between about AD 900 to 1500, left many examples of pottery decorated with human-bird figures. Siberian shamans wore bird-clawshoes, and the Hopewell Indian shaman would decorate his robes with bird-claw shapes cut out of mica. In China, Taoist monks were called 'feather scholars', which reveals their original role. In Ireland, the Celtic Druids were believed to be able to take wing through applied magic. While North American shamans most often identified with the eagle, the ancient Indian text 'Upanishads' calls the out-of-the-body spirit or soul 'the lone wild gander'; and the image flies from the tropics to the Arctic Circle, for geese figure prominently in Eskimo accounts of magical flight.

COSMIC CROSSING POINTS

The spirits, as we've seen in the accounts of healing techniques, for example, move in straight lines. Thus, the lines on the landscape and the straight flight of the shaman's spirit are almost certainly versions of one and the same thing. Whether the lines on the landscape ('They look like roads, but they are not roads') were put there to guide and protect the travelling spirit – a kind of safety net for the soul – or were put there to celebrate and consecrate shamanic flight, or were a record of these journeys in spirit, we shall probably never know.

But these various threads running through magical and religious lore, and the various clues at the ancient sites themselves, all point to the conclusion that the sacred centres were shamanic centres, with the life of the Universe – the Earth Goddess, the Sun, the Moon – focused upon them and throwing into relief their significance as crossing points between this world and that of spirit. And it seems clear that the lines radiating from them or linking them were highways of the soul in its out-of-the-body flight. The lines may well have been intended also as markers and guides for the spirits of the dead. The association between death and the ancient places is too strong, and the cultures that built them were too comprehensive in their symbolism, for there to be no connection.

A witch flies above the rooftops. The image is a buried folk-memory of the days when Scandinavian female shamans were said to be able to fly, and were pictured riding the sky on broomsticks.

The other mysterious aspects of the sites now fall into place. The pictures on the ground at Nazca, and the effigy mounds in Ohio, were made to be seen during an out-of-the-body experience. Again, we shall probably never know for sure whether they were seen purely in the mind's eye of the entranced and drugged voyager, or if his soul did literally wing its way along the leys and spirit paths laid out on the ground.

The geological abnormalities of the ancient centres too begin to make sense. Not only did the 'earthlight' effects around them, created by the anomalies in the Earth, proclaim them as unusual, but the enhanced magnetism or radioactivity of the stones in turn catalysed the trance of the initiated. Paul Devereux, who pioneered this interpretation of the ancient sites, speculates in *Earth Memory*:

'We can perhaps envisage the megalithic shaman, in an altered state of consciousness, lying or sleeping in head-contact with the stone of power at a site. This might have helped to engender special visions… in the way that [the Welsh holy man] St Byrnach … used the magnetically anomalous Carn Ingli to "speak with the angels".'

MAGIC JOURNEYS AND MODERN TIMES

In Europe and much of Asia, the early tribal societies that built the ancient sites developed into more complex forms. Shamans became priests, and the priests became kings. But they did not lose all their old associations with the old shamanic world.

The connection between the straight lines of spirit and the holy office of kingship can still be seen in a word like 'ruler' in English, which means both a straight-edge and a political chief. The word derives from an ancient Indo-European word, reg, which means 'movement in a straight line'. From the same root we also get the Latin *rex* (king) and thence the English 'regal'.

Look about the land, and one will see other relics of shamanic lines in regal institutions. Royalty has always surrounded itself with architecture that bristles with ceremonial ways, boundaries, royal routes and imperial avenues. Even the ceremonial ways of kingless Washington DC are laid out in straight lines. In London, the Mall is the broad way leading to and from Buckingham Palace. A sense that a straight way symbolizes a special power associated with rulership has thus survived.

Buried in the folklore of modern Western societies are other relics of the shaman's magic journey. The cosy image of Father Christmas flying in his reindeer-drawn sleigh through the magic midwinter night is a jolly version of the flight in spirit of Arctic European and Siberian shamans. The tribes there were reindeer herders. Their minds grew wings with the aid of the hallucinogenic fly agaric fungus – whose distinctive red and white cap is the colour of Santa Claus's robes. It may be significant, too, that Santa Claus lives at the North Pole – the axis of the world.

Another relic of the shaman's magical flight is the witch flying on her broomstick. Medieval witches took 'flying ointments' or 'witches' salves', which were made from hallucinogenic herbs that also created the sensation of flight by generating an out-of-the-body experience. The broomstick is an echo of the world tree; it also recalls the habit (still practised in the Americas) of sweeping clean the spirit paths on the ground to make the space sacred. The archetypal image of the witch may come from a Scandinavian sect of women shamans who practised a form of prophecy, known as seidhr, while in trance. They wore feathered garments to indicate their ability to fly when in this altered state of consciousness. They, too, were often pictured flying on broomsticks.

As a final provocative footnote to this labyrinthine tale, there is a strong hint in the Norse mythology that it was actually women who first taught men to 'fly'.

The world is a stranger place than it seems – an even stranger place than it already seems.

HOW LONG HAVE THEY BEEN HERE?

On a bright summer's day an ordinary man witnessed an extraordinary sight. Kenneth Arnold's cautious reports unwittingly launched the age of the flying saucer. His was only one in a long series of inexplicable sightings.

At about 7 p.m. on the evening of 2 April 1991, Dick Feichtinger was driving to work in Faribault, Minnesota, when he saw a curious, white, long and narrow rectangular object apparently hanging in the sky above the town. 'It seemed to be hanging up and down. Rather than horizontal it was vertical,' he told reporter Paul Adams of the Faribault Daily News. 'The fact that it wasn't horizontal is strange... the configuration and the way it was hanging, that was what drew my attention to it.'

Still more remarkable was the fact that the object was there again when Feichtinger returned home from work late in the evening. Now, instead of being simply white, it was red and green. Once home, Feichtinger, naturally somewhat excited and more than intrigued, urged his wife and children to come and look at what he had seen. His family rushed to join him. As the Feichtingers watched, the object hanging mysteriously in the sky changed colour from red and green to solid white. By this time, neighbours had come out to see what the fuss was about, and were equally astonished to see the weird rectangle in the sky – which, they later agreed, 'seemed to be intelligently guided'.

At this point something very strange happened: two aircraft came cruising incredibly low over the houses. Said neighbour Steve Kelly: 'I thought they were going to land on my house.' And they were flying extremely slowly – so slowly that Dick Feichtinger commented: 'I couldn't figure out what was keeping them up there.' Undaunted, he waved at them as he stood under a street light, and one of the planes seemed to acknowledge the wave by briefly turning on a set of floodlights – possibly its landing lights.

Before long, more aircraft were on the scene. Some witnesses said they counted up to 11 planes, including helicopters and two large aircraft. When the local military were contacted, however, they had no knowledge of any aircraft in the area besides a pair of National Air Guard C-I30 Hercules cargo planes – one of which, spokesman Lt. Kevin Gutknecht admitted, had indeed turned on its landing lights, although why was not explained. However, the C-I30 pilots did not report seeing any strange lights in the vicinity of the town. A puzzled Lt. Gutknecht was reported as saying: 'I have no idea what it is. It doesn't sound like anything we have in the Minnesota military inventory.'

This case has all the ingredients of a certain kind of classic UFO sighting. There is the bizarre light in the sky, changing colour but seemingly under intelligent control, witnessed by a number of independent observers, none of whom apparently has any reason to lie, let alone organize a neighbourhood conspiracy. There are unexplained terrestrial aircraft associated with the sighting. The military deny all knowledge, as usual, although they give away a tantalizing and inexplicable detail: why did the Hercules pilot turn on his landing lights?

The role of the military in UFO lore is a subject on its own, but this case, like the hundreds of others reported each year, serves to illustrate that the UFO phenomenon is as strong as it ever was. But how long have UFOs been seen in our skies?

SUPER INTELLIGENCE

The modern history of UFOs is traditionally considered to begin in 1947, when Idaho businessman Kenneth Arnold saw nine weird disks of light flashing through the air while he was flying over the Cascade Mountains in Washington State, USA. This extraordinary encounter is worth recounting in detail, for it is a key episode in any attempt to understand what UFOs are – and what they have been. For Arnold's experience was by no means the first recorded instance of unexplained aerial objects and ordinary humanity coming into contact with each other. The

Harry S. Truman, US President during the first sightings of 'flying saucers' after World War Two. Truman publicly stated his belief that UFOs were from outer space, and some ufologists believe that he instigated research into the phenomenon – research that remains super-secret even today.

great difference between his and previous sightings was the interpretation that was very soon put on it – that the lights Arnold saw were extra terrestrial craft.

Hardly anyone in the Western world was immune to this belief. Even US President Harry S. Truman could say, at a press conference on 4 April 1950, 'I can assure you that flying saucers… are not constructed by any power on Earth.' Just a few years later, in June 1954, at another conference in Innsbruck, Austria, Dr Herman Orberth – often called the 'father' of the German V-2 rocket, precursor of all the spacecraft launched from Earth – stated his conviction unmistakably: 'These objects are conceived and directed by intelligent beings of a very high order. They probably do not originate in our Solar System, perhaps not even in our galaxy.'

Whether or not UFOs are indeed material craft from outer space, messengers from alien civilizations, or the vehicles of galactic 'guardians' of humanity – or possibly even evidence of something far less benign that has a presence here on Earth – is a question that still vexes experts. The important point for the moment is that in the late 1940s, there was no other interpretation that made sense to most observers. Yet this was not Kenneth Arnold's own belief, and was certainly not the way that earlier witnesses saw the strange and bewildering lights and seemingly solid objects that from time to time have filled the skies throughout history and at the same time have filled the witnesses, too, with awe and wonder.

FLYING SAUCERS

Kenneth Arnold unwittingly launched the age of the flying saucer on the clear sunny afternoon of 24 June 1947. He was an experienced pilot, and that day was flying east across the Cascade Mountains from Chehalis to Yakima, Washington.

Arnold had been enticed by the offer of a $5,000 reward to spend an hour or so during his journey searching for a C-46 transport aircraft belonging to the US Marine Corps that had recently come down near Mount Rainier with 32 men on board. The Callair aircraft Arnold was flying was specially designed for working in the mountains. He took off from Chehalis airport at about 2 p.m. and made straight for the plateau of Mount Rainier.

Arnold was in the midst of his search at an altitude of about 9,200 ft above the town of Mineral (about 25 miles south-west of the peak of Mount Rainier), and was making a 180° turn when 'a tremendously bright flash lit up the surfaces of my aircraft'. Understandably startled, Arnold thought at first that he was about to collide with another aircraft. He spent an anxious half-minute or so searching the sky for the source of the flash of light, but the only other plane in the vicinity was a Douglas DC4 airliner, which he judged to be on the airlane from Seattle to San Francisco. Arnold then figured that he had seen the flash of the sun on the wings of a close flying fighter; he thought he had been buzzed by a gung-ho young USAF lieutenant in a P-51, better known as the North American Aviation Mustang, the most powerful piston-engined fighter then in common service with the USAF.

Before he had time to start searching for a fast-moving Mustang, however, Arnold saw another flash – and this time saw where it came from. 'I observed,' he reported drily, 'far to my left and to the north, a formation of very bright objects coming from the vicinity of Mount Baker, flying very close to the mountain tops and travelling at tremendous speed.' Watching the craft near Mount Rainier, Arnold at first thought that he was watching a formation of nine jets at, he calculated, a distance of over l00 miles. 'What startled me most at this point was… that I could not find any tails on them.'

The formation was flying almost directly across Arnold's own flightpath, which made it easy to make a rough calculation of the objects' speed, using the clock in his instrument panel, Mounts Rainier and Adams as markers, and reckoning the formation would pass about 23 miles in front of him. Arnold was amazed to discover that the nine craft were travelling at over 1,700 mph – an astonishing speed for the time (it was only later that year that the sound barrier, about 750 mph, was first broken by a jet aircraft). What made this phenomenal speed all the more extraordinary was the way the craft were flying, Arnold said: ·

'They didn't fly like any aircraft I had seen before… they flew in a definite formation, but erratically… their flight was like speed boats on rough water or similar to the tail of a Chinese kite that I once saw blowing in the wind… they fluttered and sailed, tipping their wings alternately and emitting those very bright blue-white flashes from their surfaces – At the time I did not get the impression that these flashes were emitted by them, but rather that it was the sun's reflection from the extremely highly polished surfaces of their wings.'

By the time the nine craft had flown beyond the southernmost crest of Mount Adams, Arnold had decided to abandon his search for the missing C-46 and make for Yakima to report what he had seen. Landing there at about 4 p.m., Arnold told his story to an airline manager and discussed it with other professional fliers, before taking off once more for Pendleton, Oregon. The news had travelled ahead of him: among the crowd of people to greet him there was Bill Becquette, from the local newspaper, the *East Oregonian*. It was during this time that Arnold described the craft he had seen as flying 'like a saucer would if you skipped it across the water'. This description was slightly garbled by Becquette, who thus originated the phrase 'flying saucers'. Then, with other pilots, Arnold cautiously recalculated his estimate of the UFOs' extraordinary speed. But even the most conservative reckoning still put their velocity at over 1,350 mph. From talking to other airmen, Arnold was now convinced that he had seen a flight of guided missiles, 'robotly controlled'. He concluded that the government had chosen this way to announce the discovery of 'a new principle of flight'.

Then the story broke, put out on the Associated Press wire by Bill Becquette. For three days at Pendleton Arnold was besieged with enquiries. Finally, exhausted and unable to work, Arnold flew the 200 miles across the state line to his home in Boise, Indiana. It was shortly after arriving there that Arnold had a telephone call from Dave Johnson, aviation editor of the *Idaho Statesman*. That conversation changed everything for Arnold. As he put it:

'The doubt he displayed of the authenticity of my story told me, and I am sure he was in a position to know, that it was not a new military guided missile and that if what I had seen was true it did not belong to the good old USA. It was then that I really began to wonder.'

ALIEN CRAFT

Arnold might well have wondered, for in the three days that he was being harassed by newshounds he discovered that his was by no means the only, or even the first, sighting of such mysterious flying objects. ('I thought it wouldn't be long before there was one of these things in every garage,' he commented wryly, at the stage when he still believed that he had seen a flight of government-sponsored machines.)

In April 1947, a meteorologist tracking a weather balloon saw a saucer-shaped object fly by – a neat irony, as so many later UFO sightings have been explained away as, and sometimes have really been, misidentifications of weather balloons. On 5

May, a 'silvery object' was reported to have dropped out of the sky over Washington State and disintegrated before reaching the ground. On 12 June, shortly before Arnold's own experience, another chain of UFOs was seen over Weiser, Idaho, and on 14 June a pilot named Rankin also observed a flight of ten saucer-like objects flying in triangular formation. At about the same time as Arnold saw 'his' flying disks, a prospector in the Cascades also witnessed a similar group of UFOs, whose presence made his compass needle go wild. Arnold's sighting in fact took place in the midst of a major UFO 'flap' – a flurry of sightings – in the late spring and summer of 1947. Between the beginning of June and 16 July that year, the US authorities received over 850 reports of UFOs from all over the USA. By September, the USAF had set up Project Sign to evaluate the reports and, among other things, consider the possibility that these were extraterrestrial craft.

What made Arnold's report different was that it sparked an equally monumental flap in the media – whose underlying assumption throughout was that 'flying saucers' were indeed alien craft, and were probably not very friendly.

Curiously enough, Arnold himself did not share this view of the origins of UFOs. In 1962, in the magazine *Flying Saucers*, he published his own conclusion: 'the so-called unidentified flying objects that have been seen in our atmosphere are not space ships from another planet at all, but are groups and masses of living organisms that are as much a part of our atmosphere and space as the life we find in the depths of our oceans. The only major difference [is] that they have a natural ability to change their densities at will.'

Arnold, perhaps, was not a man of his age; but this was not the first time that UFOs had been identified with living things in the sky. On the other hand, the belief that they were nuts-and-bolts machines was not entirely new, either.

MACHINES OF DEATH

Probably the earliest report of a UFO on record is to be found in (of all places) a treatment of architecture and civic planning called the *Samarangana-Sartradhara*, an ancient Indian text that dates back at least to 500 BC. In this, one passage describes curious machines called vimanas, which can fly, and are controlled by pilots. There follows a number of lengthy descriptions of how the vimanas' various power systems work, but they are tantalizingly obscure. The same devices are also mentioned in the great Hindu epics in Sanskrit, the *Mahabharata* and *Ramayana*, where they are described as military machines with the range to 'carry death' anywhere in the world – an assertion that, like so many aspects of unexplained and paranormal phenomena, raises as many questions as it answers. One researcher has even gone so far as to say that 'we cannot but be struck [when reading these works] by the modernity of certain passages, where we seem to be reading an account of a nuclear war'.

Roman writers noted visitations by UFOs: Livy (59 BC–AD 17) described a sighting in 214 BC at Hadria in Italy that looked like an altar in the sky, while Pliny the Elder (AD 23–79) refers to 'gleaming beams in the sky' in his *De Rerum Naturae*, and describes how in 66 BC a 'spark' fell from a star to the Earth, became as large as the Moon, and then – shrinking in size – returned to the sky. And in his *Historia Naturalis*, Pliny makes an intriguing assertion:

'A light from the sky by night, the phenomenon usually called "night suns" was seen in the consulship of Gaius Caecilius and Gnaeus Papirius and often on other occasions causing apparent daylight in the night. In the consulship of Lucius Valerius and Gaius Marius a burning shield scattering sparks ran across the sky at sunset from east to west.'

The fascinating part of this passage is the words 'usually called'. Pliny seems to assume that 'night suns' were, if not commonplace, at least well-enough known to have a common name. And, although he was one of the first naturalists, Pliny was enough a man of his time to accept such wonders without comment.

The literature of medieval Europe abounds in UFO reports of various kinds. Among the earliest are to be found in the works of St Gregory, Bishop of Tours in France in the 6th century. In his *Historia Francorum* ('History of the Franks'), the saint related how in AD 584 'there appeared in the sky brilliant rays of light which seemed to cross and collide with one another', while the following year 'in the month of September, certain people saw signs, that is to say rays or domes such as are customarily seen... to race across the sky'. Elsewhere he describes 'golden globes' that, on several occasions, flashed at speed across the skies of France. St Gregory also wrote seven volumes concerning miracles and - in keeping with his devout Christianity – seems to have been in little doubt that these were heavenly signs. The interpretation, in short, fitted the preconceptions of the chronicler.

In the same way, in AD 793, the *Anglo-Saxon Chronicle* reported: 'In this year terrible portents appeared in Northumbria, and miserably afflicted the inhabitants; these were exceptional flashes of lightning, and fiery dragons were seen flying through the air.' The Chronicle was written by secular scribes, and their report reflects the still thickly pagan atmosphere of 8th-century England – for both people and places were far less orthodox in their Christianity than the monasteries of France had been two centuries previously. What today would have been called a UFO or even a 'flying saucer' was to them a dragon. It flew in the air, it lit up the sky, and it was fearsome and inherently inexplicable; it was a dragon because that was the nearest thing in human knowledge to match what people actually saw. This unconscious mental process also helps to explain why diehard sceptics, confronted with a UFO, will always believe they have seen the planet Venus, or a weather balloon – indeed, anything other than an inexplicable and possibly alien craft.

Just as people see UFOs today, people saw dragons then. Kenneth Arnold was not the first to suggest that UFOs, in the most literal sense of being unidentified flying objects, were members of the animal kingdom. In England in 1113, a group of churchmen from Laon in France were going from town to town in Wessex (south-west England), bearing with them relics of the Virgin Mary, which they used to perform miracles of healing. At the coastal town of Christchurch, Hampshire, they were astonished to see a dragon come up out of the sea, 'breathing fire out of its nostrils'. There are plenty of reports of modern UFOs rising out of the sea, as well.

The 12th-century chronicler Ralph Niger recounts that on 9 March 1170, at St Osyth in Essex, south-east England, 'a wonderfully large dragon was seen, borne up from the Earth through the air. The air was kindled into fire by its motion and burnt a house, reducing it and its outbuildings to ashes.'

Dragons and UFOs show some interesting parallels. Whatever form UFOs take, they are always perceived as being on the very edge of human knowledge as it exists in any particular era, including some alluring extras that we can imagine but cannot (yet) achieve – such as faster-than-light travel today, or heavier-than-air flight in the Middle Ages.

Like UFOs today, dragons were familiar as ideas, but were also regarded as 'impossible' in practical terms. To the medieval mind, dragons occupied a strange no-man's land between reality and imagination. Most people had not seen one – though they might know someone who had, or who knew someone else who had. But everyone was familiar with dragons and what they did (which was guard treasure, breathe fire and fly), and everyone knew what a dragon looked like. Medieval people would have had no difficulty in identifying one if it landed in a bustling market place and snorted smoke and flame. But actual dragons remained elusive and magical, neither quite real nor quite imaginary, possible but improbable. Today, most of the same things could be said about UFOs, except that they are only magical in the sense that they are 'otherworldly' or paranormal.

An astonishing aerial battle breaks out over the city of Nuremburg on 4 April 1561. A contemporary account speaks of a 'very frightful spectacle', in which luminous globes, crosses and tubes appeared to fight one another for about an hour in broad daylight.

AERIAL CONFLICT

As time went on, and the old Anglo-Saxon myths disappeared from memory in an England conquered by the Normans, the identification of UFOs with dragons faded too. The persistent appearance of inexplicable lights and objects in the sky did not fade with them, however. In his Historia Anglorum ('The History of the English'), another English chronicler, Matthew of Paris, tells how at sunset on 24 July 1239, 'a great star like a torch appeared. It rose in the south and climbed the sky giving out a great light ... it left behind it smoke and sparks. It was shaped like a great head, the front part was sparkling and the back part gave out smoke and flashes.' And in his memoirs the French Duke of Bourgogne recalled that on 1 November 1461, an object appeared in the sky 'as long and wide as a half-moon; it hung stationary for about a quarter hour, clearly visible, then suddenly... spiralled, twisted and turned like a spring and rose into the heavens'.

Such accounts were not limited to Europe: records of strange lights over Japan go back at least to the 10th century, while in May 1606 the former capital of Japan, Kyoto, saw a succession of fireballs in the sky. One of them hovered near the Nijo castle in front of a host of witnesses, spinning like a red wheel.

And so the records continue: blue, black and blood-red balls, along with disks and blood-red crosses and two huge cylinders, battled together in the skies over Nuremberg, Germany, on 4 April 1561, and there was a similar aerial conflict a little more than five years later over Basel, Switzerland, between black spheres: 'many became red and fiery, ending by being consumed and vanishing', wrote the 'student in sacred writings and the liberal arts', one Samuel Coccius, who reported the weird events of 7 August 1566 in the city's gazette.

A SKY OF FLAMES

In the centuries that followed, observers, including the astronomer Edmund Halley (1656–1742), continued to note a host of bizarre aerial phenomena. But now the tone of the reports starts to change yet again: as the so-called 'Age of Reason' dawned in the late 17th century and rigorously 'logical' scientific observation became the order of the day, so different explanations for sightings of what we would now call UFOs began to creep in to the accounts. At Sheffield, England, on 9 December 1731, for instance, at about 5 p.m., Thomas Short saw what he later described as 'a dark red cloud, below which was a luminous body which emitted intense beams of light... the light beams moved slowly for a while, then stopped. Suddenly it became so hot that I could take off my shirt even though I was out of doors [this in the dead of winter!]. This meteor was observed over Kilkenny, Ireland, where it seemed like a great ball of fire. It was reported that it shook the entire island and that the whole sky seemed to burst into flames.'

In the afternoon of the next day, local manuscript records show, this 'meteor' appeared over Romania: ' there appeared in the west a great sign in the sky, blood red and very large. It stayed in place for two hours, then separated into two parts which then rejoined, and the object disappeared towards the west.' To the Romanian mind of the time, this was 'a sign'; to the cultured gentleman of Augustan England, it was a 'meteor', if a very strange one by our modern standards of judging meteors. The tendency to interpret such events according to the most easily available existing explanation – and one that at the time was the most acceptable socially – is even clearer in another account from 18th-century England.

On 18 August 1783, a small crowd of the gentry that included Dr James Lind (whose pioneering dietary work resulted in the eradication of scurvy from the Royal Navy), the renowned water-colour painter Thomas Sandby and the scientist Tiberius Cavallo, were on the terrace at the royal residence of Windsor Castle enjoying the summer evening when, according to Cavallo's account published the next year by the Royal Society, at about 9.45 p.m. they 'suddenly saw appear an oblong cloud moving more or less parallel to the horizon. Under this cloud could be seen a luminous object which soon became spherical, brilliantly lit, which came to a halt... This strange sphere seemed at first to be pale blue in colour, but its luminosity increased and soon it set off again towards the east. Then the object changed direction and moved parallel to the horizon before disappearing to the south-east... the light it gave out was

Many ufologists have concluded not only that UFOs are alien, but that the US government has retrieved crashed saucers like this one (artist's impression), which allegedly was taken to Fort Riley, Kansas, in November 1964.

prodigious; it lit up everything on the ground. Before it vanished it changed its shape, became oblong, and at the same time as a sort of trail appeared, it seemed to separate into two small bodies. Scarcely two minutes later the sound of an explosion was heard.'

To the scientist Cavallo the group had clearly witnessed a meteor: the proof was in the explosion, presumably made as the thing crashed to earth. The astonishing thing to modern eyes is the similarity between the cloud and the object beneath it seen in 1783, and the almost identical nature of the other so-called 'meteor' that visited England, Ireland and Romania some half a century before. But a person trained to look out for meteors will see them when something like one appears in the sky, however remotely like an actual meteor it may seem from our later perspective.

THE ALIENS HAVE LANDED

True to form, the next century saw another, no less consistent, interpretation of unexplained aerial phenomena. The Victorian era saw an astonishing leap forward in works of engineering, especially in transport – from the spread of railways around the globe to the introduction of iron steamships capable of crossing the Atlantic, and the production of the first cars. Land and sea had been conquered: but not the air. Airships seemed the most promising means of achieving sustained, controlled flight, but the major problem was power. It was not until light, compact internal combustion engines appeared in the late 1890s that airships became truly practicable. By then, they were being discussed everywhere – both as the next great advance in engineering, and as something more strange.

On 6 November 1896, the citizens of Sacramento, California, were amazed to see a light moving sedately through the night sky, apparently carried by a cigar shaped craft. During the month further reports of this machine poured in from all over California. From March 1897, the American Great Lakes states and Texas were plagued by reports of lights in the sky, some like 'electric arc lights', others shaped like balls or wheels, that were attached to a huge craft - which was at once dubbed an airship – shaped like a cigar, an egg, or a barrel, and apparently powered by propellers. On a number of occasions these machines landed, and the occupants, who appeared to be ordinary human beings, spoke to bemused witnesses on the ground. Then, at the beginning of May 1897, the reports dried up.

An airship as large as the objects that witnesses described would have had to be rigid, or it would have been uncontrollable. But it was not until 1900 that the development of rigid airships – 'dirigibles' – began, and that was in Germany. No airship then flying, either in the USA or elsewhere, was capable of the feats performed by these machines - if that is what they were. The first dirigible to fly in the USA was Thomas Baldwin's California Arrow, which took off from Oakland, near San Francisco, California, in 1904.

In August 1946, the Swedish authorities received nearly 1,000 reports of mysterious rockets in their skies, some of which crashed spectacularly into the country's inland lakes. One theory was that the Soviets were testing captured German V-2 rockets – which, in the public eye at least, were the most advanced technology of the day. But Swedish aviation engineers, who by then had considerable knowledge of the V-2, failed to find any plausible explanation. Similar displays of rocket-like behaviour by mysterious aerial objects were reported early the following month by British Army units in Greece, especially around Thessaloniki. Midway through September they were seen in Portugal, and then in Belgium.

THE WATCHERS IN OUTER SPACE

UFOs have been seen in the form of dragons, meteors, airships, rockets… and as 'flying saucers'. To the sceptic, all these bizarre sightings are either natural phenomena, errors of perception or plain hallucination. Some, perhaps most, UFO sightings certainly are no more than that. There is certainly good evidence that many truly strange lights in the sky are the

Flying saucers have been seen in the skies for a long time by many people. Although they have been spotted in various shapes, a pattern seems to have emerged in the forms of craft witnessed around the world. The most popular type is the disc shape as photographed here.

product of little-known and rarely seen natural forces, which seem to be released in areas of geological disturbance – along fault lines in the Earth's crust, for example. Such a theory may well explain a proportion, at least, of the long history of mysterious airborne lights over Japan, which is notoriously prone to earthquakes. But these explanations don't account for the UFO phenomenon as a whole.

The common belief since Kenneth Arnold's sighting in 1947 has been that UFOs are extraterrestrial craft built by a civilization that is technologically far in advance of our own. There are very strong grounds for questioning this assumption but it remains a possibility. Some of the people who claim to have spoken to aliens and extra-terrestrials also maintain that this civilization has been watching the Earth for a very long time. Presumably, there have been occasions when – for reasons we can only guess at – they have been unable to conceal their presence entirely. Or perhaps they have deliberately shown themselves, as part of a centuries-long programme of gently introducing themselves to us. In either case, when they have been obliged or have chosen to reveal themselves, they have come in clever disguises: just far enough within the bounds of human understanding, carefully matching the mood of the times, to be acceptable, if strange – and just far enough beyond normality to deter unwanted investigation or interference.

And we may just be living in the age when they decide to reveal their true purposes to us.

MESSENGERS FROM OUTER SPACE

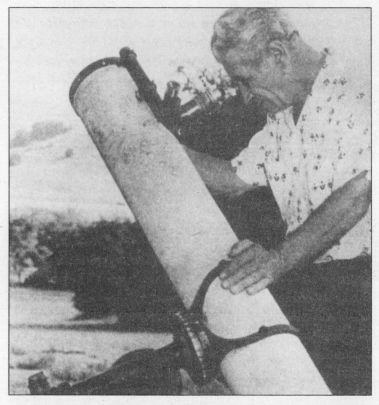

George Adamski had spent years observing the skies on the lookout for UFOs. An impulse drew him into the desert where a figure beckoned him from the opening of a ravine... but with a sudden chill of fear he wondered whether his long vigil had been wise.

Is someone – or something – inhabiting the Solar System besides ourselves? Are they out there watching us, for some mysterious purpose of their own, or are they simply our elusive neighbours? Are they friendly or are they hostile?

The answers to these questions – the most perplexing and, many would say, the most crucial in the whole debate about UFOs - should have become apparent in the decades since UFOs first revealed themselves as inexplicable flying disks. For in that time numerous people have claimed to have had direct contact with the occupants of UFOs. One might expect a clear picture to emerge from these undoubtedly traumatic experiences of who the aliens are, where they are from, and what – if anything – they want. Yet cases of contactees, and more especially those of people who have been abducted by UFOs, present some of the most conflicting and perplexing evidence of all the vast array of data in the field of ufology.

There are, essentially, three kinds of witness who might help answer some of the fundamental questions.

First, there are those people who have come so close to UFOs that they have seen and described the occupants.

Second, there are those who have been approached by aliens in a friendly spirit and have come away with what amounts to 'a message for mankind' – not necessarily of enormous cosmic import, but at least containing some explanation of what the aliens are doing and why they are here.

Third, there is a small group of people who seem to have been forcibly abducted by aliens. These cases are the most difficult to assess and contain the most astounding claims: that the contactees were subjected to some kind of medical examination, for example, and in some cases were sexually used or abused.

EVADING CAPTURE

One of the most frustrating aspects of the UFO enigma is the inconsistency of the evidence. This is particularly apparent in the descriptions of alien beings given by those who claim to have seen them.

The first such contactee to come to public attention was George Adamski, a part-time caterer who described himself as a 'philosopher and teacher' and who lived in Palomar Gardens, on the southern slopes of Mount Palomar, California. Adamski's passion was astronomy; he had a 15in and a 6in reflector telescope set up at home to watch the stars. He was also convinced that the other planets of our Solar System were inhabited. On 9 October 1946, while watching a meteor shower from his home, he saw what he later believed to be confirmation of his conviction. Along with others he saw 'a gigantic space

Adamski, with John Nebel and the 'mother ship' and attendant saucers he claimed to have photographed in March 1951.

craft' that was 'hovering high above the mountain ridge to the south of Mount Palomar, toward San Diego'. It was 'a large black object, resembling a gigantic dirigible'.

In his book *Flying Saucers Have Landed*, Adamski reports that he was first alerted to the possibility that this was 'a ship from another world' by a military officer, shortly after this sighting. From then on, Adamski spent hours every day on the lookout for another UFO. Between the winter of 1949–50 and the summer of 1952, he photographed a number of UFOs both with and without his 6in telescope, some 18 of the photos being of high quality. Adamski began giving lectures on UFOs and extraterrestrials to various interested groups, and as a result of these contacts began to hear rumours that flying saucers had been landing in 'various desert areas not a great drive from Mount Palomar'.

On 20 November 1952, Adamski, his secretary Mrs Lucy McKinnis, and the proprietor of Palomar Gardens, Mrs Alice K. Wells, met up with four such contacts – Mr and Mrs Al C. Bailey of Winslow, Arizona, and Dr and Mrs George H. Williamson of Prescott, Arizona – on the highway near Blythe, California, to go into the desert in the hope of seeing a UFO land. Adamski gives no reason for having chosen this day rather than another, but admits to following a hunch as to where they should start their vigil – about 11 miles down the highway from Desert Center toward Parker, Arizona. The group was richly rewarded.

After a stroll and a light lunch, the party sat scanning the sky. The only thing of note was the passage of a two-engine plane apparently on a routine flight. Then: 'Suddenly and simultaneously we all turned as one [sic] looking again toward the closest mountain ridge where just a few minutes before the first plane had crossed. Riding high, and without sound, there was a gigantic cigar-shaped silvery ship, without wings or appendages of any kind.'

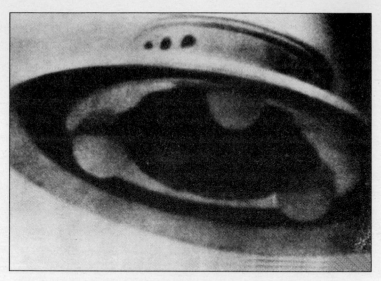

The extraordinary craft, Adamski maintained, flew over his house in Palomar Gardens on 13 December 1952. Surprisingly, no other witnesses reported the event.

The craft moved as if drifting in the direction of the group, then stopped, hovering. Adamski felt that the ship had come specifically for him, and on another hunch demanded to be taken down the road – the spot they were in, next to a well-travelled highway, was too conspicuous, he thought, and would discourage a landing.

With Lucy McKinnis at the wheel and Al Bailey accompanying, Adamski was driven off the highway onto a dirt road, while all the time the giant ship followed them silently. After half a mile or so they stopped. Here, Adamski set up his smaller telescope and a camera and then, fearing the presence of his companions would deter the aliens, sent them back to their original parking spot, to watch from there. As they left, a number of aircraft – presumably fighters – roared into sight and tried to circle the huge craft above. In response, the ship 'turned its nose upward and shot out into space'. Wondering if the planes had chased it away for good, Adamski settled down to wait.

Before five minutes was up, he saw a flash in the sky and 'almost instantly a beautiful craft appeared to be drifting through a saddle between two of the mountain peaks'. It settled on a ridge, and Adamski took photographs. Then it lifted and flew back across the saddle, as two more aircraft came into sight, circled, and flew on. Apparently the saucer had evaded them. After some minutes Adamski realized that a man was beckoning him from the opening of a ravine about 450 yds away. Wondering who this was, Adamski made his way toward the figure. Only when he was within arm's length of the man did Adamski realize that he was looking at a visitor from another world.

A WARNING

'The beauty of his form surpassed anything I had ever seen,' he wrote later. That form was unmistakably human. The man was about 5 ft 6 in tall, weighed about 135 lb, and appeared – in earthly terms – to be about 28 years old. He had shoulder-length, sandy-coloured wavy hair 'glistening more beautifully than any woman's I have ever seen'. His skin was the colour of a suntanned Caucasian's. His face was round, and he had an extremely high forehead, 'calm, grey-green eyes' that slanted slightly at the corners, high cheekbones, and a 'finely chiselled' nose. He seemed to be beardless. The alien was wearing a single-piece, finely woven chocolate-brown suit with no visible fasteners or pockets, but with a broad waistband and a close-fitting high collar. His shoes were ox-blood red and had blunt toes. Adamski thought the outfit was a uniform of some kind.

His attempts to speak to the creature failed, but by concentrating his efforts Adamski succeeded in communicating with a mixture of hand signals and telepathy. The first thing the alien told Adamski in this manner was that he was from the planet Venus. The Venusians were here, he said, because they were concerned about radiation from atomic explosions: too many of these explosions would destroy all of Earth.

And so it went on. The saucer which brought the Venusian – who did not divulge his name – to Earth had been launched from within the atmosphere by the giant 'mother ship' that Adamski had seen earlier. The craft was powered by 'magnetism'. Asked if he believed in God, the spaceman replied yes, but observed that Venusians lived according to the laws of the Creator and not the laws of materialism as Earthmen did. People from the other planets in the Solar System – all of which were inhabited – and from other systems too, were visiting Earth. Some of their craft had crashed on Earth, shot down by 'men of this world'. Saucers landed only in remote places to avoid panicking people, but the time would come when they would land near centres of population. There were many aliens living in our midst already, and for this reason the Venusian refused to be photographed, lest his features become recognizable. All aliens were essentially human in form.

Adamski was then allowed to approach the saucer hovering nearby, but was not permitted inside it. After this, the Venusian climbed aboard his craft, and it glided silently away.

DESOLATE OF LIFE

It is interesting, to say the least, that as Earth's own space programme developed during the 1960s, and probes reported with monotonous regularity that our neighbouring planets were incapable of supporting life as we know it, so the occupants of UFOs have stopped claiming to come from our Solar System. They would certainly feel uncomfortable on Venus, which has an atmospheric pressure 94.5 times higher than our own –

which alone would cause any Venusian lacking massive pressurized body armour to explode the moment he set foot on Earth – while temperatures are commonly around 900°F (five times hotter than the boiling point of water). Venusian rain consists largely of hydrochloric and sulphuric acid, and the 'air' is almost entirely carbon dioxide.

'A giant leap for mankind' – one of the Apollo 11 crew on the Moon. As human knowledge of the Solar System became more accurate and detailed, visiting UFO occupants stopped claiming to have come from neighbouring planets and made more and more extravagant claims.

However, bearing in mind that one of the few consistent aspects of the UFO phenomenon is its habit of staying just within the borders of the human imagination, it makes some sense for an alien to suggest that he comes from a place that the apparently rather backward terrestrials can immediately recognize as habitable. And in 1952 many people did believe that Venus could support life. Even then, they were wrong – for as early as the 1920s scientists had deduced that Venus could either support 'only low forms of life... mostly belonging to the vegetable kingdom' or was a desert planet plagued by dust storms. By 1932 the Venusian atmosphere was known to be mainly carbon dioxide. This meant that even vegetation was absent.

By 1975, hardly anyone in the Western world was ill-informed about space: six years earlier, the first attempt to put men on the Moon had succeeded brilliantly, while a host of unmanned craft had been sent out to explore remote space, sending back extraordinary pictures of the Solar System along with a mass of information about its planetary environments. All were clearly desolate of any known forms of life.

AN INSANE SOCIETY

Just after 2 p.m. on 28 January 1975, a one-armed farmer named Eduard 'Billy' Meier was walking near his home at Hinwel, in the canton of Zurich in Switzerland, when he saw a silvery, disk-shaped craft swoop down out of the sky with a strange throbbing sound and land about 100 yds away from him. Intrigued, he began to run toward it, but some invisible force halted him after about 50 yds. A figure then emerged from the disk, which was about 25 ft in diameter, and approached him. When it and its vehicle departed an hour and 45 minutes later, Billy Meier knew he had met a cosmonaut from the Pleiades star

An artist's impression of an encounter with ufonauts that occurred near Cennina, Arezzo, Italy, on 1 November 1954. Note the craft – few real UFO encounters conform to the 'flying saucer with little green men' stereotype.

cluster (of which seven are visible to the naked eye), 430 light years away from the Sun in the constellation of Taurus.

In all, between January 1975 and April 1978, Meier met five Pleiadians – Semjase, Ptaah, Quetzal, Plaja and Asket – in 105 encounters, photographed their five different types of flying disk on numerous occasions, and took 3,000 pages of notes on their conversations and general wisdom. According to Meier, the Pleiadians look like terrestrial Scandinavians, although their lifespan stretches to the equivalent of 1,000 of our years. They came from a planet named Erra 'in the system of Taygeta' in the Pleiades, and before that from a planet in the constellation of Lyra, from which they had emigrated millions of years previously. They had reached Earth thousands of years ago, as part of a continuous programme of space exploration, in ships capable of travelling faster than light through 'hyperspace'. Their general message for mankind was that we should concentrate on the arts of peace and cultivating the life of the spirit – otherwise, Earth was 'an insane society rushing headlong to our own destruction'. The Pleiadians communicated with Meier both through telepathy and by speaking his own dialect.

By astronomical standards, the Pleiades is young: a mere 150 million years old. Its 500-odd stars are virtually all 'B' type – ferociously hot, very large blue stars that burn themselves out very rapidly – most, in fact, have already consumed most of the hydrogen in their cores. In contrast, our Sun, a relatively cool, slow-burning 'G2' yellow dwarf, is some 4.49 billion years old, and it took a further 2.5 billion years or so before conditions on Earth were able to support even the most primitive forms of life. The chances that any planet in the Pleiades is habitable are about zero.

Assuming that extraterrestrial entities of some kind did make contact with Meier, one can only conclude that they were lying about their present galactic address. The obvious question is: why? And if they lie about that, why should we take anything else they say seriously?

The claims made by the aliens in the Meier case are as incredible as those in another, almost equidistant in time between Adamski's encounter in California and the events in Switzerland, that occurred in New York State. On 24 April 1964, farmer Gary Wilcox of Newark Valley, Tioga County, noticed something shiny about 800 yds away, among some trees on a hill where he was working. He drove his tractor up the hill, dismounted, and approached a cigar-shaped object that was hovering just off the ground.

Wilcox kicked it. It felt, he said, like metallic canvas. Then, out from under it, came two 4 ft tall but otherwise featureless creatures who, in the conversation that followed, claimed to be Martians. After an innocent conversation in which the two entities made two predictions that turned out not to be true (one foretold the death of astronaut John Glenn within the year), they departed in their noiseless, 20 ft long craft. This occurred at a time when no space scientist believed that any life form more complex than bacteria might be able to survive in Martian conditions.

VOLUPTUOUS FORMS

These contacts were elaborate and detailed for those who experienced them. They also contain elements of absurdity, illogic and falsehood on the part of the interstellar visitors, but one of the more surprising facets of ufology is the frequency with which these occur. The veteran ufologist and former editor of the internationally respected journal *Flying Saucer Review*, the late Charles Bowen, once offered his readers a few of the choice messages that ufonauts offer to witnesses.

For instance, in 1968 two beings with transparent legs handed an Argentinian farmer's son a written message that translated as 'You shall know the world' and was signed 'F. Saucer'. In 1964, a Venezuelan contactee, confronted by a pair of creatures who were hardly inconspicuous, in that they stood between 7 and 8 ft tall and sported long yellow hair and bulging eyes, asked – with commendable wit, in the circumstances – if any other 'human beings' like them were living on Earth. The reply was 'Yes. Two million, four hundred and seventeen thousand, eight hundred and five.'

Perhaps the most surreal of these utterances came in 1954, when a Frenchman came across a glowing, saucer-shaped UFO, in front of which was standing a diminutive entity who kept repeating, in a mechanical tone: *'La verité est refusée aux constipés'* ('Truth is denied to the constipated'), and *'Ce que vous appelez le cancer vient des dents'* ('What you call cancer comes from the teeth').

If these beings, who seem habitually to lie about their origins and occasionally make obscurely hilarious observations to the humans they meet, are indeed aliens visiting Earth from other planets, one would expect some consistency at least in their appearance. In fact, they take many more forms than the voluptuous young man who greeted Adamski, or the shapely Nordic blondes of Meier's acquaintance. And they are by no means as friendly or concerned for our welfare as the beings that Adamski and Meier met.

A HEADLESS FIGURE

Walter Andrus, director of the Mutual UFO Network, studied thousands of contactee cases and concluded that there were four major categories of UFO occupants. These were: small humanoids; 'experimental animals'; human-like entities; and robots. ('Little green men', the staple mocking term of the media, however, are hardly ever seen in real UFO contacts.) But these broad categories blur a multitude of differences found from one witness's report to the next.

The term 'human-like entities' encompasses extremes as far apart as the two gigantic beings seen filling a sphere as tall as a two-storey house over the Canary Islands on 22 June 1976; the blue, scaly-skinned, 6 ft tall creature that confronted 19-year-old Maria Eliada Pretzel in Córdoba, Argentina, on 13 June 1968; the creature inside a UFO seen by William Bosak near Frederic, Wisconsin, in December 1974 that had a tan-coloured, furry body, a flat nose and mouth, protruding eyes and 'calf-like' ears; and the truly nightmarish creature that in

November 1976 emerged from a UFO near Winchester, England, and stared into a car in which Joyce Bowles and Terry Pratt sat in terror: the thing was human in all visible details but for its eyes, which were entirely pink, with neither irises nor pupils, and luminescent.

The animal forms can be unexpectedly horrible. In 1960, during a UFO sighting at Yssandon, France, giant white maggots were seen crawling across a road. On 16 November 1963, two couples walking near Sandling Park in Saltwood, Kent, saw a bright golden oval UFO come down from the sky and then hover among some trees nearby. A figure emerged and approached them, but the foursome fled when it was close enough for them to make out its features: it was entirely black, had wings like a bat, and no head.

Betty and Barney Hill, whose abduction aboard a UFO in 1961 has been the subject of innumerable analyses. None has entirely explained what the couple experienced, or why they were apparently chosen for alien experiment.

Perhaps the most common form taken by UFO occupants is the classic 'small humanoid' – figures on which Steven Spielberg based both 'ET' and the creatures seen emerging from the giant spaceship in *Close Encounters of the Third Kind* (for which Spielberg used the late Dr J. Allen Hynek, a global authority on UFOs who invented the title phrase, as a consultant). Even these pale, huge-headed, hairless, soft-eyed and innocent-looking entities, which so much resemble human foetuses, vary enormously in detail, according to the witnesses' reports.

They may stand from 1 to 5 ft in height. Their eyes may be like ours, or slitted like a cat's. Sometimes they appear apparently naked; at other times in shiny black, yellow or blue garb, possibly with a cloak. Some have pointy ears, others none. Betty and Barney Hill, of New Hampshire, believed that in 1961 they had been taken aboard a craft belonging to such creatures (who were clothed in black) and given medical examinations; while in August 1990, five such beings, of various heights, apparently without clothes and with grey skin, and with only three toes on each foot, were seen walking along a main highway in Puerto Rico by numerous witnesses, but made no attempt to molest anyone. These did have the virtue of slightly resembling the creatures seen at Rio Piedras, Puerto Rico, on 3 March 1980, when teenagers Vivian and José Rodriguez surprised two pointy-eared creatures who were clothed and had webbed feet.

On other occasions, such creatures have paralysed witnesses with lightbeams from their craft – or their eyes – or physically attacked people in daylight. In the hair-raising episode experienced by Lorenzo Flores and Jesús Gómez near Carora, Venezuela, on 10 December 1954, a band of humanoids tried to drag Gómez away until his companion retaliated with his shotgun (the pair were on a hunting trip).

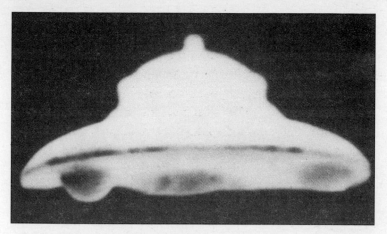

'Typical' flying saucers, like these, in fact make up a minority of real UFO encounter reports.

Most bizarre of all the perceived occupants of UFOs have been the so-called robot figures, and possibly the weirdest of all were reported by Jerry Townsend, a radio station employee from Minnesota. On the evening of 23 October 1965 he was driving toward Long Prairie when his car's electrical systems went totally dead and the engine stopped. In front of him on the road was a V-2-style 'spaceship', between 30 and 35 ft tall and resting on the tips of three fins, that might have featured in any 1950s sci-fi movie. Undaunted, Townsend got out of the car to investigate and saw, coming from beneath the rocket, three ludicrous objects walking towards him. They were no more than 6 in tall, reeling like drunken sailors on two fins, and shaped like beer cans. When they halted, a third, rear fin descended to keep them upright. In due course they tottered back to their antiquated 'rocket' and it took off – which part of the incident was also witnessed by two hunters who were some distance away.

RED RAIN

Sitting on a shelf in the microbiology laboratory of Sheffield University is a small phial containing some strange red fluid. Although to the untrained eye, the liquid appears cloudy and uninteresting, one group of scientists believe that this phial contains the first samples of extraterrestrial life.

The fluid itself was left over from one of the most peculiar incidents in recent meteorological history, which took place on 25 July 2001. In Kerala, in western India, blood-red rain fell over a period of two months. As the strange scarlet rain fell, it not only stained people's skin and clothing it also burnt the leaves off the trees. Although initially it was presumed that the rain was red because of dust swept up by winds across Arabia, a physicist at the Mahatma Gandhi University in Kottayam, after gathering samples of the rain, claimed that this theory was complete nonsense. He said that when he looked at the particles under a microscope, it was obvious they were not dust particles but that they clearly had a biological appearance. He believed that the rain was made up of a kind of bacteria which had probably been swept to Earth from a passing comet.

Of course not everyone was convinced by his analysis, and it would be fair to say that most researchers thought his idea was highly dubious. However, those researchers that believe in his work are following up on his studies. They found out that shortly before the first red rain fell there was a loud sonic boom that shook the houses in Kerala. The logical explanation for this would be that a piece had broken off from a passing comet, and that it had headed towards Kerala shedding microbes as it travelled.

Although many scientists are still unprepared to accept this explanation, it should not be ruled out as impossible and it is just feasible that the red rain was the result of some sort of extraterrestrial biology.

MIND CONTROL

None of this catalogue of strangeness – which only scrapes the surface of the cases on file – suggests that the being that was encountered by George Adamski in the California desert in 1952 was representative of its type. The brutal fact is that there is no 'type' at all when one is dealing with UFO entities, and no general conclusion to be drawn from the available evidence about their intentions and still less where they come from. So what are they?

Ufologist and specialist in radiation medicine Maxwell C. Cade once suggested that UFO occupants deliberately monitored, and reflected, what was in the mind of the witness: in some cases, homing in on their fears. Thus, the sceptics' dismissal of the contactee phenomenon that 'It's all halluci-nation' may be true, but with a significant and unexpected twist. According to Cade's hypothesis, the hallucinations are generated from within the UFO, not directly by the witness.

This would explain the huge variations in the degree of sympathy or hostility that contactees encounter among aliens, as well as the bewildering variety of shapes, sizes, colours and textures the entities display. And it would also explain the quality of alien behaviour so shrewdly noted by ufologist Peter Hough – that they 'act less like "aliens" than as if they are fledgling temporary beings hastily assembled and scripted to act out a brief scenario'.

If Cade's hypothesis is correct, it has a clear corollary: whatever they are and wherever they are from, the occupants of UFOs are doing everything in their power to prevent us seeing their true forms or learning their real intentions.

ENCOUNTERS WITH THE UNKNOWN

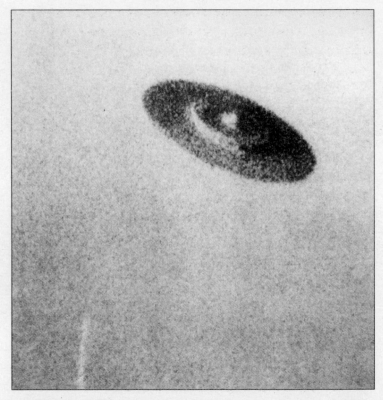

There have now been so many close encounters with UFO phenomena that it is very hard to deny their existence. Terrible injuries have been inflicted on some of the witnesses – but were these encounters with rogue military hardware, or with alien craft on a mission?

Dr J. Allen Hynek (1910–86) was one of the most dedicated, and one of the best-informed, of ufologists the world has seen. A professional astronomer, long a professor, and in due course head of the astronomy department at North Western University in Evanston, Illinois (a suburb of Chicago), Hynek was also one of those fortunate beings who always happen to be in the right place at the right time. In the late 1940s, when still in his early thirties, Hynek was recognized as a rising star (so to speak) and appointed astronomical consultant to the USAF's Project Sign, the official – if not the only – government body established to gather and assess UFO reports. Sign collapsed in 1949, its belief in the extraterrestrial origins of UFOs disbelieved and savagely discredited by the USAF establishment, to be succeeded by Project Grudge and in due course by the long-standing Project Blue Book, which was eventually wound up in 1969.

Hynek survived these political shifts and upheavals, and remained a USAF consultant right through until the end of Project Blue Book, when the USAF officially proclaimed the end of its interest in UFOs. Always, from his earliest professional acquaintance with UFOs until his dying day, Hynek rejected the extraterrestrial hypothesis – the belief that UFOs and their occupants come from some reach of space beyond this Earth – but in the course of 20 years spent investigating UFO reports on behalf of the USAF came to be convinced that something indubitably real lay behind the UFO phenomenon.

In 1984, in a brief survey of the subject, Hynek summed up his own belief concerning UFOs as follows:

'It is far from certain that UFOs represent a single phenomenon, despite the similarity in patterns of reports from all over the world… Perhaps I may presume to intrude my own opinion on these matters, based on more than 30 years of study. I believe that the UFO phenomenon is in some way directing us to consider an aspect of reality of which we have been hitherto largely unaware – an aspect, indeed, that may eventually be incorporated into our science and may prove to be of great value to the progress of mankind.'

During the International Symposium of the Center for UFO Studies (of which he was founder and director) in Chicago in 1981, Hynek confided to the author of this book that he believed that UFOs were directed by some kind of intelligence. 'That intelligence may be our own,' he added, but did not expand on his conclusion. Perhaps he felt he did not have to.

CLOSE ENCOUNTERS

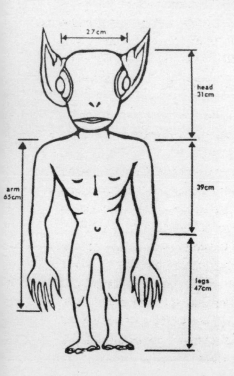

27cm

head
31cm

arm
65cm

39cm

legs
47cm

So far in this survey of the UFO phenomenon, we have seen that while there is little doubt that the phenomenon itself is real, the hard evidence that it is a physical reality is singularly elusive. The proof, in the form of a solid and indisputable example of a grounded UFO or a captured alien, does not exist.

A diagrammatic representation of one of the goblin-like entities that besieged the Sutton farm at Kelly, near Hopkinsville, Kentucky, in August 1955.

Nevertheless, UFOs of considerable size, apparent complexity and the ability to affect the environment around them continue to be seen and reported. How should one start to sort this kind of evidence?

One of Hynek's most useful contributions to the often confused debate about UFOs was a scheme for analysing the evidence: a standard and non-controversial classification of UFO sightings that any interested party could use as a starting point from which to approach the subject. Hynek divided UFO reports into two basic categories, 'distant' sightings and 'close' encounters. 'Distant' meant that the perceived object was further than 500 ft from the observer; a 'close' encounter is one that takes place less than 500 ft away from the witness.

Under distant sightings he listed three sub-categories:

(1) Nocturnal lights – which qualify as UFOs when they make unusual manoeuvres, change speed or direction, show unorthodox configurations, colours or intensity of lights, in such a way as to rule out the presence of conventional aircraft or natural phenomena.

(2) Daylight disks – unusual flying objects seen in daylight. Their shapes may be like cigars, spheres, triangles, boomerangs, eggs, and even pinpoints.

(3) Radar visuals – a comparatively rare event, when there is instrumental evidence of an unidentified object that correlates with the witness's 'subjective' report. Hynek rejected UFOs detected solely by radar because of the high proportion of 'clutter' that can appear on radar screens, especially those scanning near ground level. This distinction has perhaps become less important since many aircraft, civil and military, are now equipped with transponders that identify them individually on air traffic control and military radar screens. A consistent 'unknown' appearing in commercial or military airspace with no such electronic tag may well be a UFO.

Hynek also listed three 'kinds' of close encounter:

(1) Close encounters of the first kind: UFOs are witnessed at close quarters but do not affect the environment.

(2) Close encounters of the second kind: the UFO has physical effects on animate and or inanimate objects around it - animals are frightened, the ground is burned, electromagnetic systems such as radios or car lights and engines cease to function, and so on.

(3) Close encounters of the third kind entities are seen in or near the UFO. Initially Hynek rejected reports that people had had intelligent communication with the occupants of UFOs, and reports of abductions, as never being made by 'sensible, rational and reputable persons', but did come to accept some experiences of this kind. Such cases are now often referred to as 'Close encounters of the fourth kind' in deference to the fact that his classification has now become standard among UFO analysts.

Hynek also referred to some UFO reports as having 'high strangeness', although he never made this term part of his system of ordering as such.

THE BLACK SQUADRON

The nocturnal light is the most commonly reported UFO and is the sighting most prone to misidentification, wishful thinking or even, in extreme cases, fantasy. The number of advertising planes, their sides ablaze with some promotional message, is legion in the USA, and so is the number that have been proved to be the source of the most authentic-sounding UFO reports.

Even the most orthodox aircraft, seen at night at an unexpected angle, especially if it is large and replete with tail illuminations, landing lamps and anti-collision beacons, can become a veritable festival of light – and look very strange indeed.

Proof of alien contact and government cover-up this picture, taken in Germany in the 1950s, shows a tiny alien corpse from a saucer that crashed near Mexico City and had been sent to Europe for analysis.

Daylight disks – unless the sighting is supported by high quality photographs – can be equally ambiguous. The editor of the British partwork magazine *The Unexplained* once recounted how, in the late 1970s, he had been driving the sparsely travelled US Route 95 between Beatty and Las Vegas, Nevada, when around mid-afternoon he saw streaking across the sky an object that looked like no aircraft known to him (the son of an aviation engineer and inventor, he is familiar with a wide range of aircraft).

The craft performed no bizarre manoeuvres or aerobatics, but it was oval-shaped, with a slight bulge at the rear end, apparently wingless and tail-less, and 'the colour of dried blood'. Its speed was 'no greater than might be expected from a large, fast strike aircraft – say an F-15 Eagle – at that apparent distance. That would by most standards be very fast – the F-15 can top 1,800 mph in level flight. But there was in any case no way of knowing whether the mystery object was very small and very near, or very large and very distant; the featureless desert terrain was no help in deciding how far away the craft was, or in giving some clue as to its real size. But he was intrigued to find himself, some miles further on, passing the entrance to the USAF's Indian Springs base. Such installations seem to attract UFOs.

As it happened, the witness soon had a clue to what he may have seen: returning to Phoenix, Arizona, where he was the guest of a former USAF pilot, he learned that Indian Springs is indeed out of the usual run of USAF bases: it is the home of the USAF's 'black squadron' of covertly acquired Soviet aircraft, and over the years has been host to a number of experimental aircraft. The apparent size and, most particularly, the wingless shape and unusual colour of the object he had seen matched that of an aerofoil designed and built by NASA as part of its development programme for the space shuttle. The first shuttle was launched about a year after this sighting, so why a one-off experimental craft should still be flying, in such a location, so late in the life of NASA's programme is anyone's guess. But the point of this account was to illustrate the ambiguous nature of daylight disk sightings – even partly explained ones!

This picture of a UFO over Paris was taken by an engineer,
Paul Pauline, at around 3.45 a.m. on 29 December 1953.

HIDDEN PURPOSES

Radar/visual cases, when they occur, offer much richer pickings
to the ufologist, but they still offer no clear-cut clues as to the
nature of what has caused the sighting, or what the purpose of
the UFO may have been at the time.

At around 9 p.m. on 10 October 1990, residents around
Skibo, Minnesota, began reporting unusual lights in the sky that
were appearing to the south-east of nearby Hoyt Lakes. Two
police officers who were sent to investigate saw, as did other
witnesses, numerous objects 'of indeterminate shape,
alternately hovering and darting about'. A little over an hour after
the first reports were received, the Federal Aviation Authority's
air traffic controllers at Duluth, the area's major airport,
confirmed radar echoes from the Hoyt Lakes area, and for more

than an hour after that one of the ATCs at Duluth monitored the echoes. There were between three and five objects registering intermittently, in roughly circular formation. The local National Air Guard radar also picked up the same returns.

Further confirmation came from the pilot of a commercial aircraft flying at 11,000 ft about 45 miles west of Hoyt Lakes, who reported seeing two steady, distinct and unidentified lights at an estimated 1,000 ft below him. They were a few miles apart and a deep, glowing red. Investigators noted that no other conventional aircraft were in the area, and 'no known weather factors accounted for the anomalous radar returns'.

HARD EVIDENCE

The most spectacular UFO cases are without doubt the 'close encounters', and it is in these, especially in encounters of the second kind, that we might best be able to judge whether Hynek was on to something in speculating that the UFO phenomenon is 'in some way directing us to an aspect of reality of which we have hitherto been largely unaware'. For here, the normal and the paranormal seem to meet at an interface – as they do to a lesser extent in radar/ visual cases, but as they do not in the almost wholly paranormal and possibly entirely psychological experiences that constitute close encounters of the third kind.

This is not to say that something real does not happen in such encounters, but they are one crucial stage further removed from the everyday material world than those of the second kind. And this makes encounters of the third kind exceptionally difficult to analyse, for we are again, immediately, confronted with the old riddle about the kind of reality we are dealing with. In close encounters of the second kind we have at least a modicum of 'hard' evidence to add to the witnesses'

Close encounters of the third kind, as shown in artist's impression – a meeting between a French farmer, two entities and their egg-shaped craft in a lavender field in the 1950s.

accounts of their subjective experience. Hynek himself said close encounters of the second kind 'bear a special importance, for when it is reported that a UFO left tangible evidence of its presence… we find the real challenge to scientific enquiry'.

RED INSIGNIA

One of the classic such cases occurred at Socorro, New Mexico, in 1964 – the same town near which, in 1947, Grady L. Barnett reputedly found a crashed UFO. At about 5.45 p.m. on 24 April 1964 – a clear, sunny day with a strong wind blowing – patrolman Lonnie Zamora, on duty in the Socorro Two police cruiser, gave chase to a speeding Chevrolet. While in pursuit, he heard a brief roar and saw a flame in the sky to his right.

Zamora knew there was a shack containing dynamite in the vicinity, and his first thought was that it had blown up. He abandoned his chase and headed for the shack.

During this time the flame – blue and orange in colour, smokeless, long and narrow, and broadening toward the bottom – was descending toward the ground. The base of the flame was invisible behind a low hill to Zamora's left. Concentrating on his driving, he did not notice any object atop the flame and, besides, the sun was in his eyes.

While looking out for the shack, he noticed 'a shiny-type object to [the] south' between 100 and 200 yds off the road and below him in a gully. 'It looked', Zamora told FBI agent J. Arthur Bymes Jr later the same day, 'like a car turned upside down... standing on [its] radiator or trunk.'

Next to the object were 'two people in white coveralls... One of these persons seemed to turn and look straight at my car and seemed startled – seemed to quickly jump somewhat.' They 'appeared normal in shape – but possibly they were small adults or large kids'. Zamora radioed Sgt Sam Chavez at the sheriff's office in Socorro that he was about to investigate a possible accident, then, as he got out of the car, his radio mike fell. While he turned back to replace it, he heard 'two or three loud thumps... a second or less apart'.

Zamora approached to within 75 or 100 ft of the object, which he now saw was oval and smooth, with no windows or doors, on girder-like legs. He also noted red insignia on its side, about $2^1/_2$ ft wide. Then the roar began again, low frequency at first, rising rapidly and getting 'very loud'. The object was emitting a flame and kicking up dust. There was no sign of the 'persons' he had seen before.

Zamora thought the object might explode, and ran. The roar stopped, and he looked back to see the UFO 'going away from me in a south-west direction... possibly 10 to 15 ft above the ground, and it cleared the dynamite shack by about 3 ft'. The UFO, now travelling very fast but no longer emitting either noise or flame, rose up and sped away. It 'just cleared' a mountain in the distance and disappeared.

When Sgt Chavez arrived on the scene, he and Zamora went to investigate the spot where the UFO had landed, and where the brush was still burning. They were soon joined by FBI Agent Byrne, in Socorro on another case – and Deputy Sheriff James Lucky. They found four burn marks, and four V-shaped depressions, between 1 and 2 in deep and roughly 18 in long, in the ground in an asymmetrical diamond pattern around the burns. These corresponded to the 'legs' Zamora had seen on the mystery craft, and an independent engineer's analysis later declared that each would have been bearing a load of at least 1 ton to press so deeply into the dense earth of the district. Five other, smaller marks nearby were labelled 'footprints'. All these marks were photographed the following day.

Hynek arrived in Socorro on 28 April to investigate the sighting on behalf of the USAF's Project Blue Book. His first task was to establish the truth of Zamora's testimony, and that he could not fault. At his instigation, the USAF checked – to no avail – whether any aerospace company had been privately developing such a craft. The USAF did not, however, follow up Hynek's request that they attempt to trace the car driver who told the manager of a gas station on US Highway 85 (since superseded by Interstate 25) that he had seen some kind of aircraft just south of town, obviously in trouble and landing – and a police car was approaching it.

Sceptics have had some difficulty in trying to dispose of the Socorro case, imputing motives for a hoax to the town's mayor and suggesting that otherwise Zamora saw a 'ball of plasma' and imagined the rest. The USAF initially thought that a lunar exploration module, then being developed, was somehow responsible, but no such vehicle resembles what Zamora saw; Blue Book finally classified the sighting as 'unidentified'. Hynek himself concluded that 'a real physical event' occurred in Socorro that day.

HYSTERICAL WITH FEAR

A less celebrated but no less intriguing case occurred in England three and a half years after the events at Socorro. Sometime between 1 and 2 a.m. on 6 November 1967, Carl Farlow was driving his truck on the A338 trunk road between the villages of Sopley and Avon in Hampshire. He was approaching a junction when his lights died. The truck's diesel engine (which does not depend on an electrical ignition system) kept running and, assuming a simple short circuit of some kind, Farlow pulled up to investigate.

Before he could climb down from the cab, he was astonished to see a bizarre egg-shaped object move from right to left across the road in front of him at about 25 ft from the ground. It was magenta-coloured, with a white base, and was perhaps 80 ft long – big enough to overhang both sides of the road as it passed, exuded a smell 'like a drill boring through wood' and made a sound 'like a refrigerator'. As it crossed the road it accelerated gradually, then disappeared.

Farlow then realized that a Jaguar sedan, which had been coming in the opposite direction, was stranded on the other side of the UFO's path. Its driver, who was a veterinarian, approached Farlow, explained that his vehicle was out of action and his lady passenger hysterical, and suggested they call the police. The police arrived at the scene shortly afterwards. Their preliminary inspection of the site showed that the surface of the road seemed to have melted. The vet's passenger was taken to hospital to be treated for shock, while the two men were questioned first by police and later by a member of the Ministry of Defence.

Next day, Farlow returned to his truck. A bulldozer was at work levelling the road, the phone booth was being repainted, and other people seemed to be investigating the area with instruments. A week or so later, taking the same route in his truck, Farlow saw that some 70 yds of that particular stretch of road had been resurfaced.

BURNT BY RADIATION

Betty Cash, Vickie Landrum and her seven-year-old grandson Colby Landrum were driving home to Dayton, near Houston, Texas, on the evening of 29 December 1980, after a meal in nearby New Caney. Around 9 p.m. the trio, with Betty at the wheel, were on Highway FM1485, which runs through a forest of oak and pine. Then, Colby pointed to a bright light moving over the trees ahead of them. The light grew larger and larger – until it became 'like a diamond of fire', in Vickie Landrum's words – while every so often flames burst from beneath it. Suddenly, it was right in their way.

Betty braked hard. The three watched as the UFO hovered above the road about 60 yds away. From treetop level it sank to within 25 ft of the highway, gave out a blast of fire, and rose again. It did this several times, mesmerizing the car's occupants. They actually climbed out to see the object, which was lighting up the trees and the highway all around it, more clearly. It seemed to be made of dull aluminium, and the four points of its diamond shape were rounded. A row of blue dots ran across its centre. Now and then it emitted a beeping sound. A terrific heat was coming from the UFO, and Colby begged his grandmother to get back in the car. She and he both did, but Betty stayed outside until the object moved up and away. The car was now so hot that she could not touch the door with bare hands. Then a crowd of helicopters appeared. 'They seemed to rush in from all directions,' said Betty. 'It seemed like they were trying to encircle the thing.'

They drove on another five miles to where they could see the UFO in the distance, and the swarm of helicopters around it. One, a giant, twin-rotor CH-47 Chinook, roared right over them. They counted a total of 23 machines of various types apparently in pursuit of the clearly visible UFO.

But worse was to follow. Over the next few hours, the trio developed painful swellings and blisters on their skin and had severe headaches and stomach upsets. Vickie's hair began to fall out. Colby suffered a sunburn-like rash. Over the following week or so, Betty's eyes also became swollen to the point that she could not see, and she had to be hospitalized. In a few weeks all three had lost some hair and were developing eye problems. Their hair eventually grew again, although it was different from their original hair. Since their experience, none has entirely recovered their former good health. Doctors said that the symptoms shown by the three victims were consistent with exposure to intense electro-magnetic radiation in the ultra-violet, microwave and X-ray bands.

Investigators later established that other witnesses could confirm the UFO's flight path and appearance, and the presence of unusual numbers of CH-47 helicopters – which are quite distinctive – in the sky that night. Yet local civil airfields and military airbases deny that such a fleet used their facilities or showed on their radar. Vickie Landrum was convinced that a secret military device run haywire was responsible for her injuries, and she and Betty Cash sued the US government for $20 million in that belief. In 1986, the case was dismissed on the grounds that 'no such object was owned, operated or in the inventory' of the US Army, Navy, Air Force or NASA.

However, what the US government has not said may be significant, for it has not been obliged to admit whether or not it knows what the object was, irrespective of who owns it. So the origin and nature of the Texas UFO – like that of all other UFOs – remains an enigma. That is precious little comfort to those it affected, or to those trying to solve the mystery of UFOs as a whole. The Texas UFO case is perhaps the most baffling and frustrating of modern times, for what starts with solid evidence for a notoriously elusive phenomenon peters out in a maze of dead ends, official denials, and perhaps even deviousness.

Nonetheless, the three classic close encounters of the second kind discussed here show significant similarities. In the Avon and Texas cases there is a strong indication of military involvement, and it is possible, if by no means proven, that the military may have had some connection with the Socorro case – for by 1964, the White Sands Missile Range had acquired a further 883,910 acres of land that extended the range northwards, east of the town. There are certain physical similarities between the Texas UFO and the Socorro craft. And it is apparent that the authorities had no wish to admit to the existence of either the Avon or the Texas UFO – both of which involved multiple witnesses. And in all cases there were real physical effects, either on people or on the environment.

Are we dealing here with secret military hardware gone wrong, bursting disastrously into public gaze? Or were the UFOs alien craft that were busy trying to escape military scrutiny? Or – the wildest scenario of all, but one that some ufologists take seriously – was the military already well aware that the craft were alien, and simply trying to hide their knowledge, or even their collusion with the UFOs?

UFOS: THE PHYSICAL EVIDENCE

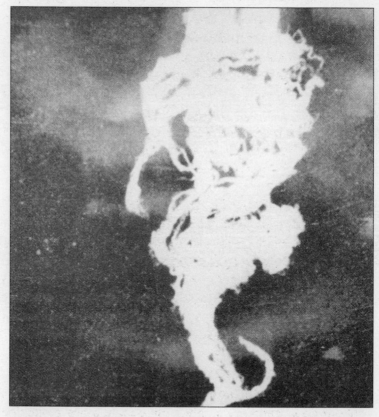

Evidence of UFOs is dramatic and varied but too often the trail goes cold. Are the scientists being silenced? And, if so, is the controlling force a human mind or something far more powerful?

The three cases considered in the last chapter demonstrate that one part at least of the UFO phenomenon involves actual hardware – since we have to assume that only physical, mechanical objects have the capacity to melt road surfaces, crush compacted, dried-out desert earth, and maim witnesses.

It is also clear from that evidence that these cases do not really illuminate ufologist J. Allen Hynek's remark late in his life that 'the UFO phenomenon is in some way directing us to consider an aspect of reality of which we have been hitherto largely unaware – an aspect, indeed, that may eventually be incorporated into our science and may prove to be of great value to the progress of mankind'. Nor do they bear out his belief that close encounters of the second kind 'bear a special importance, for when it is reported that a UFO left tangible evidence of its presence... we find the real challenge to scientific enquiry'.

For here were three classic close encounters that seem to be all too real in worldly terms to indicate that some other order or aspect of reality is involved (although it may well be in other kinds of encounter, of course). Scientific enquiry bore very little fruit in the two American cases. If it was permitted in the English case, the scientists involved were clearly silenced by the Official Secrets Act. What they already knew, or what they discovered – if anything – is still under wraps.

The manner in which the scientific trail peters out in these cases is typical of the UFO phenomenon as a whole: the most promising clues to at least part of the phenomenon are leads only to dead ends. Even when investigators are presented with quite dramatic evidence, or material that can be put into a laboratory and analysed, the conclusions raise as many questions as they answer. Not the least baffling aspect of the physical traces that UFOs leave behind is that they are as

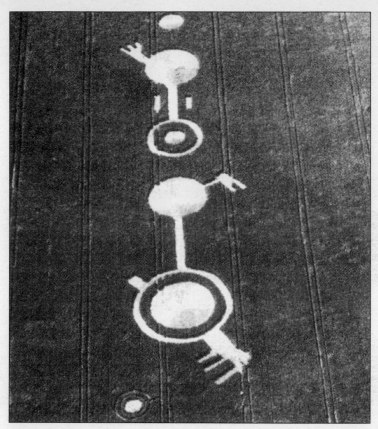

Crop circles were once taken to be UFO 'nests' or landing sites.

varied as reports of the appearance of UFOs and their extraordinary occupants – as the following, necessarily brief, survey shows.

ANGEL HAIR

French ufologist Aimé Michel recounted this instance (of many on record) of the gossamer-like material called 'angel hair' that has occasionally fallen from the sky during a UFO sighting.

At about 12.50 p.m. on 17 October 1952, a M. Prigent, the headmaster of a school at Oloron, France, was having lunch with his family when they saw a small fleet of UFOs and a 'mother ship' flying a zigzag course. The latter was a white cylinder, apparently tilted into the sky, at an estimated altitude of 8,000 ft. Travelling in pairs ahead of it were some 30 spherical objects that, M. Prigent saw through binoculars, were red spheres with yellow planetary rings around them, like smaller editions of Saturn. From time to time all these objects seemed to give out puffs of smoke, but they also left long trails of some other substance, which drifted to the ground. A large number of witnesses testified that for hours afterwards the material kept falling; it was gelatinous at first, but eventually vaporized and disappeared.

Scientists could offer no clue as to its nature – and, of course, could not examine it.

STEALTH TECHNOLOGY

One of the most dramatic reports of a radar/visual UFO sighting, with radical physical effects as well, hit the Russian press (including the district military newspaper *Za Rodinu*) in 1990, after a series of bizarre events at the long-range radar tracking station near the city of Samara (then called Kuybyshev) in Russia.

At 12.07 a.m. on 13 September 1990, the radar watch saw a blip 'comparable to that of a strategic bomber' at a range of 60 miles appear on their screens. The station's automatic electronic IFF (Identify Friend or Foe) system then failed, preventing the watch from identifying whether the aircraft was hostile or not. Two and a half minutes after its first appearance, the large blip then scattered into a host of smaller returns. By the time these were within 25 miles or so of the station, the largest of them was showing as a triangular-shaped object, and heading straight for the radar post. As it approached, a team of soldiers was scrambled to investigate: the thing shot over their heads, less than 35 ft up, as they came into the open. Then it stopped, hovering about 100 yds beyond a barbed wire barrier that lay less than 50 yds from a mobile, short-range radar array known as Post No. 12. There was a flash, and No. 12's paired aerials caught fire; the upper one collapsed to the ground. Later inspection revealed that all the steel parts had been melted.

Cameras can lie. This apparent formation of four UFOs was photographed by a US coastguard at the Salem, Massachusetts, Air Station in August 1952. Analysis has shown that the 'lights in the sky' are actually reflections of terrestrial lights on to the camera lens.

Witnesses – both officers and enlisted men – described the mystery triangle as black and 'smooth… not mirror-like – it was like a thick layer of soot'. Its sides were each about 45 ft long, and it was about 10 ft thick. There were no openings or portholes. The machine remained hovering for about 90 minutes after destroying the radar, while the post soldiers covered it – somewhat optimistically – with small arms. Then it took off.

After the press reports came official denials, and the announcement on 23 September 1990 that the story was a hoax perpetrated by a reporter on *Za Rodinu*. But it seems that a Soviet Defence Ministry commission investigated the site on 18 September, and removed the wrecked upper aerial of Post No. 12 for study. Unnamed military sources claimed to have examined the site of the event and seen tapes of the initial series of radar returns.

The description of both these on-screen radar effects and the craft itself suggests all the characteristics of 'stealth' technology – another instance of a UFO suddenly adopting an ultra-modern but little understood technological disguise. While the 'flash' and the destruction of the radar post could have been caused by a plane missile, it seems unlikely that an American stealth aircraft would have perpetrated such a provocation. And the USAF is the only military force known to have that kind of advanced aircraft in service.

SCORCHED EARTH

The notorious crop circles that plagued British farmers during the 1980s and early 1990s were very soon identified by some enthusiastic devotees of the paranormal as traces of UFO activity. However, the increasing elaborateness of the circles, the emergence of possible scientific explanations and finally the confessions of hoaxers have somewhat reduced the strength of the 'UFO hypothesis'. While hoaxers were certainly not responsible for all the circles, and even the scientists admit their explanation is far from complete, the evidence for UFOs in the usually accepted sense of the term being involved seems remote.

Among the commonest ground effects left by UFOs, however, is evidence of burning.

Over a period of two hours or so during the day of 8 October 1978, various members of the Sturgess family noticed 'something' in a field close to their house (the property is near Jenkins, Missouri) but thought little of it until it rose in the air. Six family members saw the object move away and meet another object; both then vanished, in broad daylight. Inspection of the site where the thing had been resting revealed a 4 ft circle of scorched grass, within which were three smaller circles burnt into the ground. Scientific analysis showed nothing unusual about the samples taken, however.

Samples of earth taken from a site at Medford, Minnesota, after a UFO was seen landing there on 2 November 1975 did, however, reveal some curious qualities. In radiation tests conducted by the Space Technology Laboratory at the University of Kansas, Lawrence, the samples showed ten times the thermo-luminescence of control samples from near the site, but appeared identical under the microscope. Dr Edward Zellner, the university's professor of geology, physics and astronomy, called these variations 'unusual' and 'an anomaly', but added: 'Like so much of the other data [that] has been obtained on the UFO phenomenon, the results... are inconclusive.'

On 30 September 1980, an extraordinary series of effects accompanied the UFO witnessed by 'Mr B', a farmhand and caretaker on a 600-acre property five miles from Rosedale,

Victoria, in Australia. At about 1 a.m., Mr B woke to the sound of the farm's cattle going wild – accompanied by 'a strange screeching whistling'. He got up to investigate. There was no wind, and the moon was out; Mr B saw a domed object about 15 ft high and 25 ft broad with a white top, showing blue and orange lights. For a while it hovered over a concrete water tank about 450 yds from the house, then came to rest on the ground 15 or 20 yds further on.

Mr B clambered on a motorcycle and drove to within 50 ft of the object. There was no effect on his machine, but the whistling from the UFO suddenly rose to deafening heights, there was a huge bang, and the thing lifted off. At the same time, a blast of hot air nearly knocked Mr B over. The UFO dropped some debris and then flew away to the east, holding a height of no more than 100 ft.

Mr B examined the site early next day. He found a ring of blackened grass, flattened in an anti-clockwise direction. Inside the ring was green grass, but flowers that had been growing there had disappeared. In a line to the east outside the ring was a trail of debris - stones, weeds and cow dung. For some days after the sighting Mr B suffered from headaches and nausea, and his watch refused to work normally. Strangest of all, the water tank over which the UFO had paused had been emptied of 10,000 gallons of water.

BIZARRE PHENOMENA

One of the most common physical reactions to a UFO is the collapse of electrical systems, radios and similar equipment in cars driven by witnesses. This is sometimes, but not always, accompanied by witnesses suffering rashes and nausea after the sighting, a medically recognized reaction to certain kinds of electro-magnetic (EM) radiation. Two cases, more than six years apart and widely separated geographically, show a weird variation on this theme.

Ronald Sullivan was driving on a long, straight stretch of road nine miles east of Bealiba, Victoria, Australia, during the night of 4 April 1966 when his headlight beams suddenly and inexplicably bent part way along their length to the right - as if they had been pieces of pipe. Sullivan screeched to a stop, and was then treated to a brilliant display of coloured lights coming from a field by the road. After that, an object rose up from the field and vanished. Sutherland had his lights checked before reporting the incident to the police; they were in perfect order. When the police investigated the site they found a circular depression about 5 ft across and 5 in at its deepest in the field. Sullivan reported that he 'did not believe in UFOs'.

Six and a half years later, something similar occurred at Taizé, in eastern France. At about 1 a.m. on 11 August 1972, a group of about 30 people gathered at the Protestant monastery there, witnessed a 90 ft long UFO hovering against a hillside opposite the building. This then gave a bizarre light display that involved apparently solid beams of light extending slowly to the ground. Four of those present decided to take a closer look, and went across the fields toward it armed with torches. After about 600 yds they came across a dark mass about 20 ft high and shaped like a haystack. When they shone their torches at it, the beams turned upwards at right angles just a foot or so from the object.

Neither case has been satisfactorily explained, although it is perhaps worth noting that the EM effects here occurred on an unusual frequency – that of visible light – rather than on the longer radio wavelengths that more commonly are affected by UFOs. Even this is not much help, since so many of the data on UFOs are concerned precisely with bizarre phenomena involving light.

MARKS OF THE MIND

The disparate forms of the different entities seen around UFOs, the variety of shapes and sizes of the craft themselves (if craft they are), the rarity and ambiguity of the physical evidence: all these suggest that the UFO is not one thing, but several – and possibly many.

How does the UFO phenomenon divide up, given the evidence we have? What kinds of UFO are there?

The first essential distinction to make is that in many cases something undoubtedly physical has presented itself to witnesses. But what kind of physical thing is it? There are six possibilities worth serious consideration:

UFOs are alien craft from planets in outer space.

UFOs are alien craft from a shy and elusive culture that shares our Earth and perhaps our Solar System.

UFOs are secret terrestrial craft, probably military in origin, which hide behind a screen of 'flying saucer myths'.

UFOs are not 'nuts and bolts' craft of any kind, but some kind of biological phenomenon – although some (those without apparent occupants) may possibly be wild creatures, while those with occupants may have been domesticated.

UFOs are natural phenomena that are related to ball lightning, plasma, and other little-understood manifestations of physics.

UFOs are intrusions, accidental or deliberately engineered, from other physical dimensions or parallel universes.

As the reported behaviour of UFOs is so varied, it is quite possible that each of these hypotheses is true for a particular set of circumstances – although some of them are more probable than others. But there is no law to say that if UFOs are physical objects, they have to be all the same kind of object.

On the other hand they may not be objects at all. Not all

UFOs leave physical traces, and many are seen by only a single witness, even over highly populated areas. So it is not inconceivable that the UFO phenomenon is an entirely psychological – even psychic – one.

However, there is another possibility. All six of the hypotheses offered here may be correct – in other words, it may be the case that some UFOs are indeed hallucinations, while some are natural physical and biological phenomena, some are alien craft, others are military in origin, and so on. Just as there is no rule that dictates that all UFOs must be physical objects, so there is no law to say that UFO sightings must be either physical or psychic events. They may be one or the other; they may on occasion even be a mixture of both, the product of an interaction between physical and psychological states, planes of being, or even dimensions.

Judging from a number of remarks that he made in private, it is likely that it was some such insight that J. Allen Hynek had in mind when he suggested that UFOs should make us 'consider an aspect of reality of which we have been hitherto largely unaware'. The UFO phenomenon is almost unique in exhibiting almost every aspect of the paranormal there is; the physical traces that we have been considering in this chapter may, in fact, be the marks left by the mind – although whether it is the human mind at work here, or the mind of someone or something else, we cannot be certain.